Relationships
of
Grace
Workbook

Resources by Chris Karcher

Relationships of Grace
Relationships of Grace Workbook
Amazing Things I Know About You
Relationships of Grace CD
Relationships of Grace audiocassette

Relationships *of* Grace *Workbook*

Spiritual keys for creating loving relationships, loving yourself, and living with meaning

CHRIS KARCHER

ADAMSKING PUBLISHING

Relationships of Grace Workbook
Copyright © 2004 by Christine N. Karcher

Published by AdamsKing Publishing
AdamsKing Publishing, P.O. Box 1043, Layton, Utah 84041-1043
Email: info@adamsking.com

ISBN 1-932356-53-3

All scripture quotations, unless otherwise indicated, are taken from the Holy Bible, New International Version. Copyright
©1973, 1978, 1984 by International Bible Society. Used by permission of Zondervan. All rights reserved.
Scripture quotations marked AMP are taken from the Amplified Bible, Copyright © 1954, 1958, 1962, 1964, 1965, 1987 by
The Lockman Foundation. Used by permission.
Scripture quotations marked NLT are taken from the Holy Bible, New Living Translation, copyright ©1996. Used by
permission of Tyndale House Publishers, Inc., Wheaton, IL 60189, USA. All rights reserved.
Scripture quotations marked MSG are taken from *The Message*. Copyright © 1993, 1994, 1995, 1996, 2000, 2001, 2002.
Used by permission of NavPress Publishing Group.

Cover design by George Foster, www.fostercovers.com.

All rights reserved. No part of this publication may be reproduced, stored in a retrieval system, or transmitted in any form or
by any means—electronic, mechanical, digital, photocopy, recording, or other—except for brief quotations in printed
reviews, without the prior permission of the publisher.

10 9 8 7 6 5 4 3 2 1
First Edition

Share Your Story

We welcome your stories, thoughts, and insight. Please feel free to provide feedback and share how *Relationships of Grace* or *Relationships of Grace Workbook* has impacted your life.

You are also invited to submit a story, anecdote, or quotation for possible inclusion in our next book, *Relationships of Grace Miracles.* This may be your own original material or something you have read that was written by someone else. Both the author and contributor will be acknowledged. A seventy-five-word biography of the author will be included. Multiple submissions are welcome. For additional information, please see the page at the back of this book entitled "Share Your Story in Our Next Book *Relationships of Grace Miracles*" or visit www.RelationshipsOfGrace.com.

Please share your experiences, stories, and reactions to *Relationships of Grace* or *Relationships of Grace Workbook* by sending them to:

feedback@RelationshipsOfGrace.com
www.RelationshipsOfGrace.com

Relationships of Grace
P.O. Box 1043
Layton, Utah 84041-1043
Fax: 801-547-0928

Contents

Preface...9

Week 1

Moonbeams of Grace...11

Yearning for Love 11

Turning Away from Love 12

A Spiritual Approach 13

What Is Grace?...14

Moonbeams of Grace 16

The Naked Choice..18

Week 2

Loving Yourself...23

The Mask, the Mud, and the Masterpiece............................27

From Fear to Love 35

Value from Birth..41

Week 3

Overcoming the Fear of Other People's Opinion 45

Darkness Into Light..51

Integrity..57

Week 4

Loving Others...63

The Holy Spirit 67

Week 5

The Golden Rule 73

Acceptance..79

Week 6

Living with Meaning..83

Passion 85

Making a Difference 91

Freedom from Illusions..95

Week 7

Dreams Come True...99

Joy in the Journey 103

Foot Washing for Grace 107

Week 8

The Spiritual Journey...111

Knowing God...113

Centering Prayer 119

Week 9

Gratitude and Grace 123

Solitude...127

Week 10

Growing Like a Child..131

On the Wings of Grace 137

Preface

Chapter headings and subheadings in this workbook correspond to the chapter headings and subheadings in its parent book, *Relationships of Grace*. For additional information and entertaining stories that illustrate each workbook topic, refer to the corresponding section in *Relationships of Grace*. When a question in this workbook refers to *Relationships of Grace*, refer to the section in *Relationships of Grace* with the same section name. For maximum benefit, use *Relationships of Grace* and *Relationships of Grace Workbook* together as companion books.

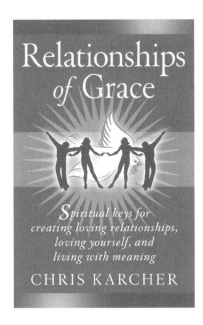 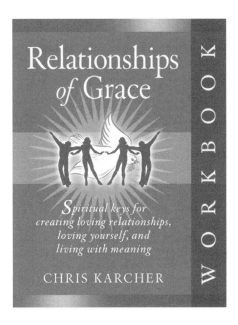

CHAPTER ONE

Moonbeams of Grace

Yearning for Love

As different as people appear on the surface, deep inside, we are the same. We hunger for love. We long for a full life and to connect with others. Meaning enters our lives through our relationships with God, others, and self. We were created to experience love through deep, meaningful relationships.

- What does every person ever born hunger for?

- Think of someone in your own life who is difficult to deal with, someone who gets under your skin. What does he or she hunger for?

- All of the Ten Commandments are laws about what?

All of the Ten Commandments are decrees about relationships.

- In ten words or less, paraphrase Jesus' teachings in Matthew 22:36–40about all the laws in the Bible.

Five words summarize Jesus' teachings about all the laws in the Bible: "Love God, neighbor, and self." (Matthew 22:36–40)

- According to Romans 13:10, what satisfies all of God's requirements?

The book of Romans explains, "Love satisfies all of God's requirements." (Romans 13:10 NLT)

We are so wonderfully made that our deepest yearning—to love and be loved—is God's desire for us.

Relationships of Grace Workbook

Turning Away from Love

Without knowing it, we turn away from love. It is offered to us every day, moment by moment. Sometimes we embrace love; other times we resist it.

It's easy to understand why. Words sting. Dreams fall apart. Hearts break. To-do lists are long. Time is short. Perhaps someone has wronged you. Maybe you have been excluded, betrayed, or unfairly judged, leaving you feeling lonely or afraid. Perhaps you are dealing with a rebellious teenager or have received disheartening medical tests results. Maybe financial troubles overwhelm you. Perhaps you harbor resentment and are finding it difficult to forgive the pain of an undeserved wound.

–   Complete the following sentences:

•   "I am angry because . . ."

•   "I am sad because . . ."

•   "I am afraid that . . ."

•   "I am hurt because . . ."

"My soul finds rest in God alone; my salvation comes from him. He alone is my rock and my salvation; he is my fortress, I will never be shaken. How long will you assault a man? Would all of you throw him down- this leaning wall, this tottering fence? They fully intend to topple him from his lofty place; they take delight in lies. With their mouths they bless, but in their hearts they curse. Selah. Find rest, O my soul, in God alone; my hope comes from him. He alone is my rock and my salvation; he is my fortress, I will not be shaken." (Psalm 62:1-6)

- "I am sorry that . . ."

Emotional turmoil creates strongholds that keep you from an intimate relationship with God and the fullness of grace.

After a lifetime of self-sufficiency, and believing all I needed to do was try harder to experience the peace and joy I longed for, I discovered the opposite is true. I let my mask drop long enough to learn, in the words of Jesus, "By myself I can do nothing." (John 5:30)

In precious moments when I remember this, I find myself immersed in the sweetness of grace.

"By myself I can do nothing." (John 5:30)

"I can't do a solitary thing on my own." (John 5:30 MSG)

A Spiritual Approach

Many people acknowledge suffering is a part of life, but you may be experiencing more frustration, disappointment, worry, and sadness than you need to. By understanding the keys to grace-full living, your life will be supremely transformed.

Relationships of Grace and *Relationships of Grace Workbook* inspire change from the inside out. They unravel the questions, how do we . . .

Teilhard de Chardin, a French theologian, said, "We are not human beings having a spiritual experience. We are spiritual beings having a human experience."

- Know God?

- Love ourselves?

- Create loving relationships with others—families, friends, coworkers, neighbors, and acquaintances?

- Overcome fear, worry, stress, addiction, or a bad habit?

- Live with a sense of meaning?

- Open our hearts to grace?

The theme of *Relationships of Grace* and *Relationships of Grace Workbook* is this: You create loving relationships, love yourself, and live with meaning by choosing to open your heart to grace. Note the two keys: grace and choice.

Grace is God's part.

Relationships of Grace Workbook

Choice is ours.

- What is God's part?

- What is your part?

What Is Grace?

"My grace is sufficient for you, for my power is made perfect in weakness." (2 Corinthians 12:9)

Grace is all of the blessings we receive because of God's unconditional love. Grace is the unmerited favor, undeserved mercy, and loving-kindness of God. It is the presence of God, actively working in our lives. Joyce Meyer defined grace on her television show, *Life in the Word,* as "God's power coming to you free of charge to do in your life, with ease, what you could never do with any amount of struggle."

- In your own words, define *grace.*

- Can you earn grace?

- Grace is the ultimate gift of God's unconditional love. What are some of the things in your life that keep you from opening your heart and accepting the gift of grace?

Our world is blanketed in grace. All of our blessings and everything good in life flows from God's grace. We could not live without grace; we are totally dependent on it. The air we breathe, the food we eat, family and friends, our talents, and

Moonbeams of Grace

tulips in springtime are all gifts of God's grace.

- How are you dependent on grace to survive?

The power of God working through you to help you change and face a challenge is grace.

- Using specific examples of challenges you face today, paraphrase Galatians 3:10.

"And that means that anyone who tries to live by his own effort, independent of God, is doomed to failure."
(Galatians 3:10 MSG)

- Referring back to your responses when you wrote about some of your emotional turmoil in the "Turning Away from Love" section, are you more likely to lean on God and ask Him for help or try to handle things yourself?

- What percentage of the time do you (a) lean on God to help you with your struggles versus (b) try to attack your problems by yourself?

- List some concrete ways you can invite God's power into your life to help you face your challenges.

Spontaneous healings, divine incidents, and deliverance from

Relationships of Grace Workbook

harmful situations are miracles of grace.

- List some "coincidences" that you now know was God actively working.

Lunch with a friend, a walk on the beach, a cozy moment before you get out of bed in the morning, and sitting in front of a blazing fire on a cold winter night are graceful experiences.

- List some common, everyday blessings that are examples of living in grace.

Even trials that provide us with opportunities for growth and turn our lives around for the good can be acts of grace.

"We also rejoice in our sufferings, because we know that suffering produces perseverance; perseverance, character; and character, hope." (Romans 5:3-4)

- What are some trials you have experienced that, looking back, you now see provided the opportunity for growth? Referring to Romans 5:3-4, explain how you grew from them.

"My grace is enough; it's all you need. My strength comes into its own in your weakness." (2 Corinthians 12:9 MSG)

- According to 2 Corinthians 12:9, what is the only thing you need?

God provides the grace and strength we need *when we seek Him*. During times of weakness, God's grace—His love, presence, comfort, and power—helps us through.

- Write a short prayer asking God to give you strength, comfort, and power to help you through the challenges you are now facing.

Moonbeams of Grace

We can reflect the beams of grace if we choose. While God is the source, we become vessels of grace when we reflect the rays of love.

- As presented in the "Moonbeams of Grace" section of *Relationships of Grace,* what is a moonbeam of grace?

- What does 1 Peter 4:10 call us to do?

> The New Testament uses the word *administer* when it teaches we should be "faithfully administering God's grace in its various forms." (1 Peter 4:10)

- It's easy to give grace to people we agree with and who are kind to us. What are some examples of how you can administer grace to others who are not so amiable? Be specific.

- What are some examples of how our schools and churches withhold grace?

- How could these institutions become vessels of grace?

Relationships of Grace Workbook

- What role can you play in helping them?

The Naked Choice

Referring to "The Naked Choice" section of *Relationships of Grace,* what was the amazing discovery Victor Frankl shared in *Man's Search for Meaning?*

Choice is key to graceful living. Your choice is whether you will allow yourself to be immersed in grace. This is an opportunity you are given moment by moment.

To experience the loving relationships you yearn for, allow yourself to be drawn into the graceful life. Every blessing you have has been given to you. Notice the gifts of grace that surround you—the extraordinary as well as the ordinary.

The Apostle Paul said, "Embracing what God does for you is the best thing you can do for him . . . fix your attention on God. You'll be changed from the inside out." (Romans 12:1–2 MSG)

- What is the key for graceful living according to Romans 12:1-2?

- What are some extraordinary—and ordinary—blessings of grace that surround you?

You open your heart to grace through a personal relationship with God—*not religion, relationship.* This is a process, not a one-time event. It involves making the choice, moment-to-moment, to enter into a relationship with God.

"Avoid the talk-show religion and the practiced confusion of the so-called experts. People caught up in a lot of talk can miss the whole point of faith. Overwhelming grace keep you!" (1 Timothy 6:20-21 MSG)

- Explain the difference between a relationship with God and the "talk-show religion" referred to in 1 Timothy 6:20-21 MSG.

Moonbeams of Grace

- It is important to understand how often we are presented with the choice to allow ourselves to be drawn into and immersed in grace. How often are you given the opportunity to choose to open your heart to grace?

To live in grace is to allow God's power to work through you. For example, during a speaking engagement, I will be nervous if I try to speak on my own and focus on myself. Will the audience like me? Will they agree with me? Will I do a good job? My stress-level is higher when I strive to remain self-sufficient.

But if I lean on God, ask Him to help me, and focus on the message rather than the outcome, my anxiety will diminish. By speaking in partnership with God (albeit not an equal one), words will be given to me. Yes, I need to practice and prepare, but I am not speaking alone. I have a Helper—which also means the applause is not mine.

- What is something in your life that causes you stress?

- In times of stress, how can you enter into partnership with God instead of remaining self-sufficient?

- What is the end result of leaning on God and asking for help?

It is freeing to realize the goal is not perfection. What's important is living into God's plan. God will give you the grace you need if you are willing to receive it.

- Paraphrase the following, "It is a blessing we do not have to be—cannot be—perfect. I am going to stop striving for perfection and start using my energy to live into God's plan instead." Elaborate with specific examples.

Relationships of Grace Workbook

- List your top 5 goals for the week.

"I'm after love that lasts, not more religion. I want you to know God, not go to more prayer meetings." (Hosea 6:6, MSG)

- According to Hosea 6:6, what two things does God want?

If you do not complete any other goals—if your house is a mess and if you missed a deadline at work——but you know and love God, God will be pleased. Similarly, if you are the top salesman in your department, your kid gets straight As, or you lead the women's group at church, but you do not know and love God, you have not lived into God's plan for you.

- Reflect back on your top 5 goals for the week. Are loving and knowing God included? Do you have any revisions you would like to make to your goals?

How do you open your heart to grace, moment by moment, through choice? Love and know God.

- Give a specific example for each of the following sentences of how you can:

- Enter into a relationship with God.

- Develop an awareness of the blessings of grace given to you.

- Move from striving on your own to allowing God's power to work through you.

Moonbeams of Grace

- Let God work His will in you.

- Ask Him for help.

- Relinquish self-sufficiency, recognize your dependence on, surrender to, and trust in God.

- Leave the outcome to God.

Know God.

Then, God will transform you. (Romans 12:1–2) He will change you from the inside out by changing your heart.

Change your heart and you change your life.

God offers you the choice, but will not choose for you. In graceful moments, the longing of the heart is satisfied. As you enter into the miracle and mystery of grace, you will create loving relationships, love yourself, and live with meaning.

You will experience relationships of grace.

CHAPTER TWO

Loving Yourself

Do you know how marvelous you are? You are created in the image of God and crowned with glory and honor.

- What do Genesis 1:27 and Psalm 8:5 teach about how you were created?

"So God created people in his own image; God patterned them after himself; male and female, he created them." (Genesis 1:27 NLT)

To be created in the image of God does not mean we are perfect or gods. God is always greater. But one of the remarkable things about grace is God loves us despite our dirt, although God doesn't always love the things we do and wants us to make healthier choices.

God "crowned us with glory and honor." (Psalm 8:5 NLT)

"I'm So Glad I'm Me"

Self-love is not to be confused with being self-centered. Self-love leads to selflessness and self-sacrifice. It does not mean "me first;" it means "me *too*." Self-love does not mean you neglect your family and friends to get what you want. It means you do not neglect yourself in the process of loving others. It is not a prideful arrogance. Humility increases as self-love grows. When you love yourself, you are more loving toward others. Your relationships are better with fewer conflicts. You are able to make healthier choices. Criticism is not as disabling. Adverse circumstances and other people's opinions do not easily sway you. You feel more joyful and at peace. Instead of resenting other people's good fortune, you can rejoice, secure in the knowledge there is plenty of grace to go around.

- Describe how and why the concept of loving yourself is consistent with Biblical teachings.

Loving yourself is Biblical. The Golden Rule and the Great Commandment to "love your neighbor as yourself" are based on the assumption you love yourself.

Relationships of Grace Workbook

Self-love develops out of a reverence for God's creation and by understanding you are valuable to your Creator, despite your flaws.

- If self-love develops out of a reverence for God's creation, it follows that self-loathing reflects a lack of respect for God's creation. Share your thoughts about this.

Our Need for Love

Mother Teresa said we are created "to love and to be loved." Love is our deepest desire, our greatest passion. Every person ever born longs to love and be loved.

Self-love is critical for healthy relationships and personal growth. Our ability to love others is directly related to our ability to love ourselves. When we do not feel good about ourselves, it impacts our relationships with others. Internal hurts wound those around us.

- Describe a time when your own internal wounds have adversely impacted your relationships with others.

- Difficulties in our relationships with others often stem from personal issues. Many personal problems can be traced to a lack of self-love. Some people fight. Others flee. Some become doormats and allow people to take advantage of them. Others engage in self-destructive activities. Which best describes you?

- Would you describe yourself as angry, critical, and unforgiving, or as someone who gives grace freely to others?

We cannot give what we do not have. When we are critical of ourselves, we are critical of others. When we are filled with rage, we lash out at others. But when we are filled with grace,

24

Loving Yourself

we are free to respond in grace to others.

People with a low sense of self-worth often feel hurt and make unhealthy choices. People who have been disabled by past experiences of abuse and abandonment have an especially difficult challenge. Some wounds are so deep that turning to God is the only way to heal.

Many people expect others to make them happy instead of accepting responsibility for their own happiness. They look to others to fill their emptiness and make them whole. How they feel about themselves is dependent on external circumstances.

- Are you overly sensitive to criticism from others? If so, give an example.

- If someone yells at you over a trivial issue, are you more likely to (circle one):

  (a) Internalize it and think something is wrong with you
  (b) Think the other person is being unreasonable and let his or her fury roll off you?

- Are you dependent on praise from others to feel good about yourself? Explain.

We all enjoy receiving the admiration of others. But if you allow praise to define you, you are relying on the opinions of others for your sense of self-worth.

Love from others is never enough. To use a common example, if you fill a bucket with water, but the bucket has a hole in it, you can pour water in the bucket all day and never fill it. You must first plug the hole.

But how is the hole plugged? How do you love yourself? That is the subject of this chapter.

Self-love grows, not through an endless search into self, but through grace—by accepting God's love and nurturing a personal relationship with Him. This means trusting in that which is greater than self and making the choice, moment by moment, to accept the gift of God's grace.

- List three examples from the previous paragraph that describe how self-love grows.

25

Relationships of Grace Workbook

- What is the key to loving yourself?

- Write your name in the blanks in the following sentences. Then, read each sentence aloud:

  - I, _____, have been created in the image of God.

  - God loves me, _____, unconditionally despite my dirt.

  - I, _____, am of value because God created me.

  - I, _____, have been given unique talents to love and serve the world around me.

  We'll explore how you can embrace your inherent value as a person created by God as we discuss:

  - The Mask, the Mud, and the Masterpiece

  - From Fear to Love

  - Value from Birth

  - Overcoming the Fear of Other People's Opinions

  - Darkness Into Light

  - Integrity

Loving Yourself

The Mask, the Mud, and the Masterpiece

The Mask

Our mask is the front we put on for others. It tries to deceive and hides the person within. It is concerned with what other people think and worries about projecting the right image to the world.

The mask tries to make us look good. It tries to show how great we are and that we are better than others. It tries to prove our worth by showing how smart, talented, and wonderful we are. Our desire to be number one, belong to the best group, and achieve power and wealth are the mask at work.

- What type of front do you put on for other people?

- What are some truths about yourself that you hide from others because exposing them would make you feel vulnerable?

The mask associates worth with doing and having. Feeling good is dependent on *doing* well in school, on the job, in sports and *having* possessions, power, control, and the admiration of other people. Unhappiness is the result of not being able to *do* or *have* something you want.

- List some specific examples of how try to prove your worth

27

Relationships of Grace Workbook

based upon *doing* and *having* as described in the preceding paragraph.

- List a goal you have that is based on external achievement— instead of intrinsic value.

- List a desire you have for a loved one because it would make you look or feel better about yourself.

The Mud

The mud is our fear, envy, insecurities, discontentment, resentment, and concern about what other people think. It is the part of us that tries to conform to the world. Unhealthy and unloving choices are made in the mud.

Self-discovery can be difficult because it exposes the truth: We all have mud. I am wedged in it up to my waist sometimes.

We try to circumvent our vulnerability by denying our emotions. Rather than feel our pain, we mask it. Some lash out in anger rather than admit they are hurt or afraid. Others try to escape by anesthetizing their pain. They turn to substitutes like shopping, alcohol, food, work, or unhealthy relationships.

But what we *want* is different from what we *need*. The cravings are for something deeper, something more.

- Describe a *want* as opposed to a *need.*

Saint Augustine of Hippo said long ago, "We keep searching until we find ourselves in God."

- What did Saint Augustine of Hippo mean when he said, "We keep searching until we find ourselves in God"?

Loving Yourself

Everything flows from this longing. Nothing else can bring us into the fullness of life.

When I am trying to "find myself," self gets in the way if my search is independent of God.

The basic component of mud is self-sufficiency. We spend a lot of time in the mud when we are out of relationship with God.

What keeps me from loving myself? Not accepting God's love. Wanting things my way instead of trusting God to provide what I need. Insisting things happen my way, on my timetable, on my terms. Trying to control other people and circumstances instead of accepting them as they are. Languishing in the mud.

–   Read Matthew 6:25-30 and complete the sentences listed below.

•   I want . . .

•   By not providing me with what I want, God has provided what I need by . . .

•   I want . . .

•   By not providing me with what I want, God has provided what I need by . . .

•   I want . . .

"If you decide for God, living a life of God-worship, it follows that you don't fuss about what's on the table at mealtimes or whether the clothes in your closet are in fashion . . . Look at the birds, free and unfettered, not tied down to a job description, careless in the care of God. And you count far more to him than birds . . . Instead of looking at the fashions, walk out into the fields and look at the wildflowers . . . If God gives such attention to the appearance of wildflowers-- most of which are never even seen--don't you think he'll attend to you, take pride in you, do his best for you?" (Matthew 6:25a, 26, 28b, 30 MSG)

Relationships of Grace Workbook

- By not providing me with what I want, God has provided what I need by . . .

The Masterpiece

The Apostle Paul wrote, "We are God's masterpiece," (Ephesians 2:10 NLT)

- How does Ephesians 2:10 describe you?

You are God's masterpiece, God's work of art.

– Write your name in the blanks in the following sentences. Then, read each sentence aloud:

- I, _____, am God's masterpiece. (Ephesians 2:10)

- I, _____, am God's work of art. (Ephesians 2:10)

Allow the masterpiece to be unveiled

How do you put down the mask and get out of the mud? How is the masterpiece unveiled?

The answer is simple. You don't unveil it. God does. Your part is choosing to accept the gift of grace and to know God.

- Read Romans 12:1-2.

In Romans, the Apostle Paul urges, "Give your bodies to God. . . . Don't copy the behavior and customs of this world, but *let God transform you* into a new person by changing the way you think. Then you will know what God wants you to do." (Romans 12:1–2 NLT, emphasis mine.)

While creating *David,* Michelangelo said it was his aim to release the angel imprisoned in the stone. God's aim is to release the angel in you and set you free from the bondage of self-sufficiency.

To "give your body to God" is to give all of yourself to Him. Instead of conforming to the world, put God at the center of your world. Then, God does the work of transforming you.

Change is through transformation, not imitation.

The mask is too tough to penetrate and the mud is too deep for you to change all by yourself. By accepting the gift of grace, you allow God's power to work in you. This helps you move from "I want what I want" to surrendering control and trusting in what God wants.

Loving Yourself

- In your own words, describe how you can allow the masterpiece to be unveiled. Write your response in first person (i.e., use "I," "me," "my").

Live as the person you were created to be

You were uniquely created with special gifts. Your strengths, the things you love to do, and the things that fill your life with meaning are divinely inspired.

Your identity is a person created by God to love and be loved, and to use your unique gifts for God's purposes.

Discovering what brings you joy includes understanding what keeps you from it. Self-destructive activities that drain your energy and prevent peace are signals that your choices are inconsistent with the desires of your heart.

- What must you do before you will know what God wants you to do according to Romans 12:1-2?

After you have entered into a relationship and "let God transform you into a new person . . . *then* you will know what God wants you to do." (Romans 12:1–2 NLT, emphasis mine.)

– Read the quote from Soren Kierkegaard's *The Prayers of Kierkegaard* and complete the sentences below.

- I experience joy when . . .

In *The Prayers of Kierkegaard,* Soren Kierkegaard said, "And now Lord, with your help I shall become myself."

- I feel at peace when . . .

Relationships of Grace Workbook

- I can nurture my spirituality by . . .

- The blessings of grace that surround me are . . .

- I have fun when . . .

- My strengths are . . .

- My weaknesses are . . .

- I would like to be remembered for . . .

Loving Yourself

- If I keep living as I am today, I will be remembered for . . .

- My top five priorities in life are . . .

- The qualities I admire in other people are . . .

- The qualities I admire in myself are . . .

- I can use my talents to serve others by . . .

- The thing I love most about my life is . . .

Relationships of Grace Workbook

During times of weakness, God provides the grace and strength we need when we seek Him. And God's grace—His love, presence, comfort, and power—helps us through.

- The thing I am most dissatisfied about in my life is . . .

- Things that drain my energy are . . .

- I am enthusiastic about . . .

- Time passes quickly when I am . . .

- Time passes slowly when I am . . .

Let God release the angel in you and set you free from the bondage of self-sufficiency. Why not try trading the mask and the mud for grace—and marvel, as the masterpiece is unveiled.

Loving Yourself

From Fear to Love

A certain amount of fear is healthy. Fear warns us of potential danger and signals us to take action in threatening situations. It is important to heed these warnings. Fear keeps a woman from walking alone at two o'clock in the morning and a child from accepting candy from a stranger. Fear of getting hurt keeps us from running out in front of a moving car. Fear of the consequences keeps us from engaging in self-destructive activities.

What triggers some of our other, less rational fear? We want to belong. We want to feel special and know we are loved. We seek power and control.

- Check the statements that apply to you.

_____ I have not pursued my passion because I fear the unknown.

_____ I work at a job I am bored with because I am afraid to leave my comfort zone.

_____ I am a workaholic because of my fear of failure.

_____ I am immobilized by criticism and fear being unloved.

_____ I boast because of my fear of not being good enough.

_____ I argue to prove I am right because I am afraid of not appearing smart enough.

_____ I react with hostility when I am afraid to admit I am hurt.

_____ I spend beyond my means because of my fear of not being held in high esteem by my friends.

_____ I indulge an addiction (overeating, shopping, alcohol, etc.) to mask emotional pain.

_____ I am afraid of becoming vulnerable and letting my feelings show.

_____ I act without integrity (i.e., inconsistent with my value system) because I fear people's opinion.

_____ I remain in an unhealthy relationship because I am afraid of being alone.

_____ I envy my friend's achievements because of fears about

"Fear not" passages are included in the Bible 366 times—a verse for every day, including leap year.

Relationships of Grace Workbook

my own self-worth.

_____ I seek power because I am afraid to release control.

We are all afraid at times—of loss of security, of loss of control, and of not being loved. We are afraid because we know along with love comes hurt.

Consequences of Fear

Fear keeps us from loving. We cannot fear and love simultaneously. Fear robs us of our peace.

- Give an example of how fear robs you of peace.

Fear keeps us from leaving the security of our comfort zone to become the person God created us to be. Fear can keep us stuck in an unhealthy relationship or in work that is inappropriate for us. Pursuing our passion and living with a sense of purpose requires us to trust God to provide what we need as we follow His will.

- How is fear keeping you from living God's plan for you?

Fear keeps us from surrendering control. Instead, we struggle for power over people, things, and circumstances we cannot control.

- How might you be trying to control another person or circumstances beyond your control?

One of the functions fear serves is to mask the person hiding beneath the surface. We are afraid of becoming vulnerable and exposing the real us. We are afraid of what people might think if they knew the person behind the façade.

Rather than admit we are hurt or afraid, we rage. We blame others, become defensive, and exile the people who threaten us.

Perhaps a bigger fear is that *we* might see past our façade. We are afraid of what we might find if we look too deep. We try so hard to project a certain image that we lose sight of who we really are. Or, perhaps we do know who we are, but we are afraid we are not of value.

- Reflect on a personality trait you have that hides your vulnerability because of a desire to mask the real you.

Loving Yourself

The irony is, along with the mud, the mask hides the most beautiful part about us. The mask hides the angel, the masterpiece longing to be unveiled.

Longings of the Soul

Much of what we do is an act of love or a cry for it. Love and hate are antonyms according to the dictionary. But the root of hatred is fear. Emotions that appear to be unloving or hateful are masking fear.

– Fear-based emotions are listed below. Write of a time you experienced each of them. After each example, note which of the following was the root cause of your fear: loss of security, fear of being unloved, fear of being powerless and out of control.

• Resentment

• Envy

• Anxiety

• Embarrassment

• Pride

• Self-centeredness

• A compulsion to control or be controlled

• Arrogance

- Defensiveness

- Insecurity

- Hostility

- Habitually proving you are right

- A compulsion to please.

The commandments to love God and one another are teaching you to follow the longings of your soul. By first seeking your deepest longing—God—you will then move away from fear and deeper into love for neighbor and self.

Fear-based emotions rob you of peace.

To grow past our fear and move deeper into love, it helps to understand who we are as individuals.

Our self-descriptions are incomplete when we seek identity through roles, activities, and accomplishments. What we *do* is different from who we *are*.

Our true identity is a person uniquely created in the image of God to "love God, neighbor, and self." (Matthew 22:36-40) Understanding who we are grows out of our understanding of God's will and by using the gifts given to us for God's purposes.

- What does Romans 12:3b teach about understanding your identity?

"The only accurate way to understand ourselves is by what God is and by what he does for us, not by what we are and what we do for him." (Romans 12:3b MSG)

Different methods of personality typing attempt to categorize people according to personality traits, highlighting vast differences among us. But among the diversity is a greater similarity: our need for love. When you walk into a room, you can already know the profound longing of every person there— a yearning for love.

Surrender control

Surrender is accepting God's will and yielding our will to His. Surrender involves trusting God without knowing the

Loving Yourself

details of His plan.

Fear keeps us from surrendering. When we are afraid, we fight. We strive to prove our worth. We struggle for security. We seek control.

- What does 1 Peter 5:7 teach you to do with fear?

"Cast all your anxiety on him." (1 Peter 5:7)

Surrender does not mean you avoid personal responsibility, give up, stay in bed all day, or become a doormat. Nor does it mean you allow another person to control you. Establish limits and resolve conflicts, but in love.

God is in control.

- What does Psalm 27:1-3 teach about surrendering control and trusting in God?

"The Lord is my light and my salvation-whom shall I fear? The Lord is the stronghold of my life-of whom shall I be afraid? When evil men advance against me to devour my flesh, when my enemies and my foes attack me, they will stumble and fall. Though an army besiege me, my heart will not fear; though war break out against me, even then will I be confident." (Psalm 27:1-3)

- Give a specific example of how you might yield your will to God's and trust Him.

Know you are equally special

You and I are part of a team—humanity. The Master Craftsman molds each of us. Each of us is specially made— uniquely created with extraordinary talents—but of equal value to everyone else.

- Can you think of a time when you tried to prove your worth by comparing yourself with others? If so, explain.

You are special to God, regardless of how special the world may or may not think you are. No matter what issues you are

Relationships of Grace Workbook

struggling with, no matter what you may or may not have accomplished, no matter what indiscretions lurk in your past, you matter to your Creator. Being better than others is not what makes you special. You are special because you are His.

Trust

When Moses was instructed to bring the Israelites out of Egypt, God said, "I will be with you." (Exodus 3:12)

- What did God promise Moses in Exodus 3:12?

After Moses' death, God commanded Joshua, "Do not be afraid or discouraged. For the Lord your God is with you wherever you go." (Joshua 1:9 NLT)

- What did God command after Moses' death in Joshua 1:9?

Moving past our fear requires us to leave the security of our comfort zone to live God's plan, and trust in Him to provide what we need.

The antidote to fear is faith.

– Fill in the blank:

- I fear _____.
  God is in control. I need to have faith and trust God.

John, the disciple, taught, "There is no fear in love. But perfect love drives out fear." (1 John 4:18)

- What does 1 John 4:18 teach us about releasing fear?

God is the source of perfect love. Love triumphs over fear in moments when we experience divine intimacy and trust in God's perfect love.

How can you fear less and love more? Trust God. Accept and administer grace, by accepting God's love and allowing that love to flow through you. Release things and place them into God's hands. When the world seems to be falling apart, the security that can come only from God will bring you peace.

40

Loving Yourself

Value from Birth

You are valuable because God created you. Not perfect, but valuable. Value is a gift of grace. You are of value to your Creator because you exist. You are not required to *do* anything for this value. You cannot earn it. You cannot lose it. God loves you because He created you.

- Write your name in the following blank:

- God delights in _____.
  (Psalm 149:4)

Value is not an entitlement. You are of value, not because you have earned your worth, but because God is love. God is always greater. God's love is so extravagant your innate value is given freely as a gift. Understanding you do not have to be perfect—cannot be perfect—but are of value anyway makes the gift of grace even more remarkable.

- Why are you valuable?

- Write some synonyms for *valuable.*

Who Me? Yes, You.

- Put your name in the blank. Read each sentence aloud, emphasizing the capitalized word each time.

- GOD loves me, _____.

- God LOVES me, _____.

- God loves ME, _____.

"God delights in his people."
(Psalm 149:4 MSG)

Beings not Doings

God's capacity to love is greater than our capacity to mess up. Yes, we are held accountable and suffer the consequences of poor choices. Self-responsibility is a major theme of the Bible, but so is the unfailing, unconditional love of God.

As we are drawn into the mystery of God, we are freed to appreciate how loveable we are in God's eyes in spite of our imperfections. Efforts to make God love us are futile because God never stopped loving us in the first place.

You are a human *being,* extraordinary because you *are.* Achievements, good deeds, and the accumulation of material possessions are not a barometer of value.

Made some unhealthy choices? Wounded by someone else's misconduct? Spouse mad at you? Mess up at work? Such issues have no effect on your worth. You are valuable.

Receive a promotion at work? Wear designer clothes? Adept at what you do? Your child at the top of his class? You are undoubtedly blessed, but your worth remains unchanged.

Your acceptance of your inherent value and God's unconditional love is key to self-love.

- Are you more valuable because of your achievements?

- Do poor choices make you less valuable?

- Why are you of value?

Understand the value of God's creation

We experience feelings of low self-worth when we fail to acknowledge that *everything* comes from God. Loving God involves loving everything God has created, including you. Self-love is not an emotional attachment to personal worth. It is reverence for that which God has created.

"So God created man in his own image, in the image of God he created him; male and female he created them." (Genesis 1:27)

- Read Genesis 1:27. Do you believe God is the creator of the universe and everything good in it, including you?

Loving Yourself

- Do you acknowledge the value of God's creation?

- Write your name in the blank.

- God created _____.

Loving yourself is a faith issue. If you believe in God as the Creator, present in the miracle of birth, your value is an inherent part of creation. To deny this is to deny the value of God's creation.

- When you are struggling with self-loathing, what does that say about how much you value God's creation?

If someone tells me, "God loves you," who is doing the loving? God, not me. If I am already struggling to love myself, it can be difficult to comprehend I am the recipient of this love.

You are loveable, not because of your accomplishments, but because of your Creator.

God loves *you* unconditionally. God breathed life into *you.* Among the splendor of the universe, God invested in *you.* God chooses *you.*

- Do you love God's creation?

Enter into a personal relationship with God

Self-love grows when you enter into a personal relationship with God and accept His love. Moment by moment, you are given the opportunity to choose whether you will open your heart to grace. This means taking the risk to be more spiritually connected by recognizing your dependence on God and surrendering control to Him.

Grace penetrates the deepest pit.

- How does self-love grow?

- How often are you given the choice to open your heart to grace and accept God's love?

Relationships of Grace Workbook

Saint Augustine of Hippo said God continually tries to give good things to us, but our hands are full.

- What did Saint Augustine of Hippo mean when he said God continually tries to give good things to us, but our hands are full?

When you allow yourself to be drawn into grace, you know God, not through knowledge but through a relationship. Pain from the past begins to heal, and you are transformed. Your love for God's creation, including love for yourself, grows. This means you don't try to earn God's love, but accept it as the gift it is.

- Describe how you can allow yourself to be drawn into and immersed in grace.

You are of value because God created you.

Loving Yourself

Overcoming the Fear of Other People's Opinion

- Answer the following questions *yes* or *no*.

_____Do you feel guilty when you say no?
_____Does criticism crush you?
_____If someone is mad at you, does it ruin your day?
_____Are you afraid other people will not like you?
_____Do you do things you don't want to do because you are afraid someone might not like you if you don't?
_____Are you afraid people will think you are incompetent?
_____During conflicts, do you cry and apologize when you are not at fault?
_____Is being "nice" more important to you than doing what you know is right?
_____Do you have trouble standing up for yourself?
_____Do you quietly seethe rather than face an issue?
_____Do you go to great lengths to win someone over who is upset with you—not because it is the right thing to do, but because you are afraid he or she will stay mad at you?
_____Is it difficult for you to assert yourself?
_____Are you a people-pleaser?
_____Do you allow others to disrespect you?
_____Do you allow others to take advantage of you?
_____Are you afraid to discipline your children for fear they might get mad at you?
_____Are you so busy pleasing everyone else you have no energy left for yourself?
_____Do you go along with things to get along when it is contrary to your value system?

Yes answers to these questions indicate circumstances in which you likely fear other people's opinions of you.

In this section we will consider ways in which you can become less sensitive to the opinions of others.

45

Relationships of Grace Workbook

Fearing Other People's Opinion

Love and belonging are basic human needs. This makes us vulnerable to the opinions of others.

We fear other people's opinions of us. We want to be liked. Most of us get anxious if someone is mad at us.

"They loved praise from men more than praise from God." (John 12:43)

– Contemplate John 12:43. Then, give an example for each of the following:

• You said *yes,* when you should have said *no.*

• You said or did something inconsistent with your value system because you feared not being accepted by others.

• In order to be "nice," you chose an unsafe behavior.

• You acted like a "wimp" instead of negotiating and working an issue.

• Suffered from burnout pleasing others while neglecting your own physical, spiritual, or emotional well-being.

The Unavoidable Problem

Jesus taught, "You have heard that it was said, 'Love your neighbor and hate your enemy.' But I tell you: Love your enemies and pray for those who persecute you." (Matthew 5:43–44)

• What is the unavoidable problem, according to Jesus' teaching in Matthew 5:43–44?

Jesus did not teach we should not have enemies. He assumed we would. Therein lies the problem. We are going to experience

46

Loving Yourself

the disapproval of others.

Growing Stronger

Your worth as a human being is in no way dependent on winning the approval of others. Disapproval does not decrease your worth. Approval does not increase it.

Our need for love and belonging is so fundamental to our existence that we will never be able to completely overcome our fear of the opinions of others. It's nice to be admired, but it is not possible to receive the approval of everyone with whom we come in contact. If a person claims to be immune to other people's opinions, he or she may be attempting to become invincible by denying the human need for love and belonging.

But you can continue growing so you are not overly sensitive or immobilized by feelings of rejection. As you grow, you will experience less emotional turmoil. Criticism will not hurt as much. Conflicts will be resolved more quickly.

Accept that a certain amount of disapproval is inevitable

- List three people you admire, who have done what is right, but have been the targets of unfair criticism.

The message? A certain amount of disapproval is inevitable. Expecting everyone to like and approve of us all the time is unrealistic.

Don't give another person power over you

Authentic power is grace, God's power, flowing through you. Your worth is not affected by the opinions of others.

- Let's explore how you can stand in the power of grace, and not yield your power to others. For each of the following examples, think of an applicable real-life experience. Then, describe how you can keep from giving your power away should the situation happen again.

- You acted in a way that was inconsistent with your value system.

Relationships of Grace Workbook

- You did not stand up for your belief system.

- You allowed someone to take advantage of you.

- You tiptoed around someone because you were afraid of upsetting him or her.

- You withdrew, sulked, wept, or lashed out in anger instead of working through an issue.

- You allowed another person to treat you disrespectfully.

- Someone treated you disrespectfully and you bent over backward to get back on his or her good side.

Loving Yourself

- You did not assert yourself because you were afraid others would disagree with you.

Change your focus from people to grace

Whenever you have a mountain to climb, God extends His hand to help you. And He is there to break your fall.

Place disapproval from others in God's hands. Ask what lesson can be learned from the situation. Focus on God's will instead of human will. You will grow from the experience. Accept the invitation to enter God's family.

- What does 1 John 4:4b teach?

> John the Disciple wrote, "The one who is in you is greater than the one who is in the world." (1 John 4:4b)

- When you are feeling rejected by a family member, what family invitation is always available?

- Instead of looking to other people for support and validation, how can you change your focus from people to grace?

In the graceful life, you place yourself in the hands of the Great Protector. Your focus changes from the people in the world to the Creator of the world.

And one day you realize you are not as afraid of the opinions of others.

Loving Yourself

Darkness Into Light

Meaning by Way of Suffering

- Who is referred to as the "Suffering Servant"?

Jesus is referred to as the Suffering Servant.

Have you ever wondered why we like to think we should not suffer? Jesus suffered.

Joni Eareckson Tada, who became a quadriplegic after a diving accident, says, "God has a plan . . . We shouldn't view life's struggles as daunting obstacles to our happiness. They can be the very keys *to* our lasting happiness, true contentment, and godly joy."

- According to 1 Peter 4:1-2, how might your sufferings be described? What is the benefit of suffering?

The Disciple Peter wrote, "Think of your sufferings as a weaning from that old sinful habit of always expecting to get your own way. Then you'll be able to live out your days free to pursue what God wants instead of being tyrannized by what you want." (1 Peter 4:1–2 MSG)

Our tendency is to look outward to other people and external circumstances for the solution to our problems. If only he were a better mate (or friend, or relative, or boss), things would be peaceful. If only circumstances were different, my problems would be solved. If only I could get the new job and a bigger house, life would be good.

- What are some examples of how you blame circumstances or other people for your unhappiness, instead of accepting responsibility?

Expectations are one of the greatest deterrents to joy. They

51

indicate we assume someone or something else is responsible for our happiness. When other people or external circumstances don't turn out as anticipated, we become hurt, angry, disappointed, or irritated. The greater the expectation, the greater the hurt.

- What are some unrealized expectations that create frustration and discontent in your own life?

"Lean not unto thine own understanding," Proverb commands. (Proverbs 3:5)

The Psalm eloquently says, "If your heart is broken, you'll find God right there; if you're kicked in the gut, he'll help you catch your breath." (Psalm 34:18 MSG)

Who can explain hardship and tragedy? According to Proverbs 3:5, we should not try to understand suffering.

- How does God's grace help you during suffering according to Psalm 34:18 and Romans 8:28?

"In all things God works for the good of those who love him, who have been called according to his purpose." (Romans 8:28)

In *The Hiding Place,* Corrie ten Boom said, "Every experience God gives us, every person he puts in our lives, is the perfect preparation for the future only He can see."

- Reflecting on Corrie ten Boom's quote from *The Hiding Place,* what struggles you have gone through that were "the perfect preparation for the future"?

The Beauty of Aging

What is the beauty of aging? Growth. Wisdom. Love. And, hopefully, trust. My friend once read, "It is not your fault if you are not beautiful at eighteen. It is your fault if you are not beautiful at eighty."

- Without making any reference to physical appearance, describe how you are growing more beautiful.

Seek grace in the darkness

One of the most surprising aspects of grace is it is often

52

Loving Yourself

hidden in turmoil. Personal hardship, frustration, boredom, irritations, encounters with difficult people, financial difficulties, and burnout can all be acts of grace. Sometimes we have to crash before we are willing to slow down.

Darkness precedes growth. Sometimes, God may bring us face to face with an obstacle until we learn. This is not to imply evil is God's will. Evil is the result of human will—free will—and wrong choices.

Problems are not hopeless situations. They are messages. Heartache and mild depression can be signals we are ready for passage into a new phase. A broken romance may indicate it was not a good match. Exhaustion is a sign to rest.

- Describe a "problem" you have experienced that, looking back, you can now see as an opportunity for growth.

Lean on God

The Apostle Paul had what he referred to as a thorn in his flesh. Paul never revealed the specifics of his ailment, but he divulged its purpose: "to torment me" and "to keep me from becoming conceited." Paul begged to have the thorn removed, but God chose otherwise.

It would have been easy for the prolific author of much of the New Testament to become arrogant and forget about his need for God. The Lord wanted Paul, not puffed up, but on bended knee—and mindful of his dependence on God. So God added a thorn to the mix.

- What did God tell Paul in 2 Corinthians 12:7–10?

Paul was most likely to turn to God during times of weakness. By relinquishing self-sufficiency and receiving grace, Paul grew stronger as he allowed God's power to work through him.

- What are you currently experiencing that challenges you to lean on God for strength and wisdom?

"To keep me from becoming conceited because of these surpassingly great revelations, there was given me a thorn in my flesh, a messenger of Satan, to torment me. Three times I pleaded with the Lord to take it away from me. But he said to me, 'My grace is sufficient for you, for my power is made perfect in weakness.' Therefore I will boast all the more gladly about my weaknesses, so that Christ's power may rest on me. That is why, for Christ's sake, I delight in weaknesses, in insults, in hardships, in persecutions, in difficulties. For when I am weak, then I am strong." (2 Corinthians 12:7-10).

The Apostle Paul said, "No test or temptation that comes your way is beyond the course of what others have had to face. All you need to remember is that God will never let you down; he'll never let you be pushed past your limit; he'll always be there to help you come through it." (1 Corinthians 10:13 MSG)

Ask, "What am I being called to learn?"

- What does 1 Corinthians 10:13 teach about difficult times?

Darkness comes before light. Pain is a signal something is out of balance and you have choices to make. By adapting a paradigm of finding the lesson, you transform problems into opportunities for learning and growth.

- Some of life's paradoxes are listed below. Note a time when you experienced each of them.

- Some good comes from bad.

- A weakness can make us grow stronger.

- A painful experience can be a powerful teacher.

- The more we give, the more we receive.

- The line between joy and pain—and love and hate—is thin.

A healthy psyche does not make you immune to grief or feelings of rejection. It gives you the courage to ask, "What might I be doing to invite suffering? What is the lesson I am being called to learn?" Paul's lesson was to learn how to keep his pride in check and rejoice in his need for grace.

- While reflecting on some of your own struggles, consider the following questions.

- What am I being called to learn from the "thorn in my flesh"?

Loving Yourself

- Am I leaning unto my own understanding instead of trusting God?

- What is the purpose or payoff of my behavior or emotions?

- What do I want that I am not getting?

- Am I so focused on getting what I want that I'm ignoring the other person's needs?

- Am I trying to control circumstances instead of accepting reality?

- Am I being trained for a future not yet known to me?

Trust God

- Think of something you have longed for but not received. How might God be giving you the desire of your heart by not giving you what you want? (Psalm 37:4)

"[God] will give you the desires of your heart." (Psalm 37:4)

- What is challenging you to relinquish self-sufficiency and trust in God's plan?

The graceful life is about trust. When you surrender, you give up control and turn things over to God. This does not mean you abdicate self-responsibility. It means you stop trying to control things over which you have no control anyway.

What keeps us from loving ourselves? Unmet expectations. Insisting things happen our way instead of trusting in God's plan. Not accepting God's love and grace. Separating ourselves from God.

Trusting is key for moving from darkness into the light.

Loving Yourself

Integrity

Relationships of Grace describes some extraordinary acts of integrity that occurred amidst the tragedy of September 11, 2001.

- What are some memorable acts of integrity you have witnessed?

What is Integrity?

Integrity is choosing your thoughts and actions based on values rather than personal gain. Ethics prevail above individual benefit. Decisions consider the best interest of everyone involved. Interactions with others are compassionate.

The prayer of integrity is God's will be done.

Dwight L. Moody, an American evangelist, said, "Character is what you do in the dark."

- What does integrity mean to you?

- Is there a secret thought or desire you have that is inconsistent with your value system?

Relationships of Grace Workbook

- In the above example, if you prayed God's will, what would your prayer be?

Integrity heals. Lack of integrity hurts. The fact that "everybody else does it" or "nobody will know" is irrelevant. Personal satisfaction, expectations, and the fear of judgment are beside the point.

Integrity is compromised any time the best interest of everyone involved is not accounted for.

- Which temptations from the list in Romans 1:28-31 are challenging you to remain in integrity?

"Furthermore, since they did not think it worthwhile to retain the knowledge of God, he gave them over to a depraved mind, to do what ought not to be done. They have become filled with every kind of wickedness, evil, greed and depravity. They are full of envy, murder, strife, deceit and malice. They are gossips, slanderers, God-haters, insolent, arrogant and boastful; they invent ways of doing evil; they disobey their parents; they are senseless, faithless, heartless, ruthless." (Romans 1:28-31)

Note that Biblically, according to Romans 1:28–31, gossip, fighting, greed, envy, and arrogance share the list with murder—with no stated hierarchy.

- How do you feel after you gossip?

- How might you reduce the amount of conflict in your life?

- How does greed impact you and the people around you?

- Who do you envy, and why?

- When engaged in conversation with others, are you more likely to talk about yourself or more likely to listen and show an interest in the other person?

Loving Yourself

Self-Respect and Self-Love

Integrity is key to self-respect, which grows when our actions are consistent with our value system. We lose self-respect when our actions are inconsistent with our values.

Self-respect affects the way we feel about ourselves. Acting with integrity increases our level of self-respect and feelings of self-love. When we lack integrity, we do not feel good about who we are; our sense of self-worth diminishes.

- Give an example of a time when you acted contrary to your value system.

- How did your behavior make you feel about yourself?

Author Mark Twain said, "Few things are harder to put up with than the annoyance of a good example."

Ungraceful Consequences

An attorney told me it is not uncommon for him to find the perpetrators of unethical business dealings in the hospital with stress-related illnesses. When you are out of integrity, your conscience records and remembers it.

What are the consequences of lack of integrity? When the clerk gives us too much change, what is the problem with keeping it? Do we really "get away with it" when we pad our expense account, gossip about our neighbor, or distort the truth?

The problem is we remove ourselves from the loving state of grace. The consequences can be painful. We experience inner turmoil: regret, anxiety, guilt, shame, and sorrow.

Our relationships with ourselves, other people, and God suffer.

- Give an example of a time when acting without integrity caused you to lose self-respect and diminished your feelings of self-worth.

People who administer lie detector tests receive Christmas cards from prisoners expressing gratitude for the relief they felt after they confessed.

When we act without integrity, we hurt our relationships with others because we lack credibility with them. People don't trust us and distance themselves from us. Feelings of guilt and shame

Relationships of Grace Workbook

may cause us to distance ourselves from them as well.

- When has acting without integrity hurt your relationships with others?

When we act without integrity, we hurt our relationship with God because our heart wants to choose God's will. To act without integrity, we either separate ourselves from God or we were not in a relationship with Him to begin with. When we are in a relationship with God, we choose integrity.

- Think about a time when you succumbed to temptation. How would you describe your relationship with God at that time?

Never allow another person to compromise your self-respect

Gandhi said, "They cannot take away our self-respect if we do not give it to them."

By choosing actions based on an ethical center, you do not allow another person to compromise your dignity and self-respect. Choice is key.

- In order to choose based on your values, you need to be clear about what your values are. Describe your value system, your "ethical center."

- How have you allowed others to influence your choices and "take away your self-respect"?

60

Loving Yourself

- Read Romans 1:28 again, this time from Eugene Peterson's *The Message*.

- According to Romans 1:28 MSG, what was the root cause of the wayward lifestyle Paul refers to in his letter to the Romans?

"Since they didn't bother to acknowledge God, God quit bothering them and let them run loose. And then all hell broke loose . . ." (Romans 1:28 MSG)

Allow the power of grace to flow through you

Living with integrity is difficult. The consequences are often painful. It is not easy to stand in truth when it may cost you something you want: for example, some extra change, a friendship, or your job.

- When have you been challenged to stay in integrity when you knew it would cost you something you wanted?

How do you find the courage and strength to live with integrity? By being filled with the power of grace, through a personal relationship with God.

Human strength is no match for the power of grace.

CHAPTER THREE

Loving Others

Living with Bears

At a management seminar I attended, the instructor asked us to list our most difficult problems in the workplace. We students called out our woes as the teacher wrote them on a white board.

The instructor stood back and reviewed the list. Relationship issues not only topped the list, they were the only problems on it. The instructor, who had taught the class for years, noted the difficulties mentioned were always people problems.

- What issues are you struggling with?

- Circle the problems you listed that are "people-problems."

Meaning Through Relationships

We long to move deeper into the fullness of loving relationships. We feel isolated and lonely without them. Unresolved issues in our relationships create turmoil. Our connections with one another bring meaning into our lives.

- Without using the word *love,* paraphrase Matthew 22:39. Use examples that reflect *love* instead.

"Love others as well as you love yourself." (Matthew 22:39 MSG)

Relationships of Grace Workbook

- Name the people who are most meaningful in your life.

- Do your actions and the way you allocate your time reflect the importance of these people?

The challenge is to recognize we are dependent upon grace for peaceful, loving relationships. Too often, we demand love rather than offer it. We grow by learning to accept and administer grace.

- Reflecting back to our study of grace in the first chapter, how do you accept and administer grace?

– For each of the following sentences, give an example of how you can deepen your relationships with those most important to you. Be specific.

- Ask God for help.

- Let God work His will in you.

- Enter into a relationship with God.

Loving Others

- Develop an awareness of the blessings of grace given to you.

- Relinquish self-sufficiency, recognize your dependence on, surrender to, and trust in God.

- Leave the outcome to God.

But how are we to cope with the bears in our lives that are attracted to the smell of garbage and rotting fish? "Don't feed the bears" literature is given to visitors in national parks inhabited by bears. Forest service rangers teach, "Respect the bears." Rangers describe black bears as shy. They attack only when they are provoked or feel threatened—precisely when human bears are most likely to attack.

- Think of someone who is difficult to deal with. How can you lean on God and allow the power of grace to work within you?

We'll explore how you create loving relationships with others as we focus on:

- The Holy Spirit

- The Golden Rule

- Acceptance

Loving Others

The Holy Spirit

Holy Guidance

God works within and communicates with you through the Holy Spirit. Because of the Holy Spirit, you are able to experience God's presence and have a direct relationship with Him.

Willpower is not enough to effect change. You need the power of grace, working through the Holy Spirit, to change.

- How does the Bible describe the Holy Spirit according to John 14:16, Romans 8:26–27, and Luke 12:12?

"And I will ask the Father, and He will give you another Comforter (Counselor, Helper, Intercessor, Advocate, Strengthener, and Standby), that He may remain with you forever." (John 14:16 AMP)

"In the same way, the Spirit helps us in our weakness. We do not know what we ought to pray for, but the Spirit himself intercedes for us with groans that words cannot express. And he who searches our hearts knows the mind of the Spirit, because the Spirit intercedes for the saints in accordance with God's will." (Romans 8:26-27)

"For the Holy Spirit will teach you at that time what you should say." (Luke 12:12)

When you listen to the Holy Spirit, you are listening in the presence of God. Father Thomas Keating, a founder of Contemplative Outreach, likens listening to the Holy Spirit to a pilot using one of the old airplane guidance systems.

Pilots navigated by following radio beacons strategically placed on major air traffic routes throughout the country. These stationary radio beacons emitted signals. A plane's navigation system picked up the beacon's signal as the plane flew toward the beacon. If the plane began to stray off course, the signal faded. By monitoring the signal strength, a pilot knew when he was beginning to veer off course and could reposition to get back on route.

The Holy Spirit is our divine guidance system. The Holy Spirit beacons us to stay on course and helps us find our way when we lose our bearings. We often look outward to others for guidance when many of our most important answers lie within, through the Holy Spirit.

Relationships of Grace Workbook

Fruit and Consequences

- According to 2 Corinthians 3:18, what happens when you allow the Spirit to work within you?

"As the Spirit of the Lord works within us, we become more and more like [Christ], and reflect his glory more and more." (2 Corinthians 3:18 NLT)

The Holy Spirit guides us to accept and administer grace.

When we don't listen to the Holy Spirit, we make a lot of unhealthy choices. Instead of being vessels of grace, we stop its flow when we don't allow God's grace to flow through us. The moonbeams of grace lose their glow. We choose poorly causing us to feel shame, guilt, and remorse. Our relationships suffer. We experience regret, hurt, and disappointment. Decisions are difficult. Our feelings of self-respect diminish.

- What is an example in your life when not listening to the Holy Spirit caused you suffering?

When you choose to open your heart to grace and enter into a personal relationship with God, the Holy Spirit will transform you.

The Lord told Ezekiel, "I'll give you a new heart, put a new spirit in you. I'll remove the stone heart from your body and replace it with a heart that's God-willed, not self-willed." (Ezekiel 36:26–27 MSG)

- What is the promise of Ezekiel 36:26–27?

- In Ezekiel 36:26–27, who is doing the transforming—God or Ezekiel?

Then, you will reap the fruit of the Spirit: "love, joy, peace, patience, kindness, goodness, faithfulness, gentleness, and self-control." Your relationships will improve. You will feel better about yourself. You will fear and worry less. And you will live with a sense of meaning, purpose, and passion.

"But the fruit of the Spirit is love, joy, peace, patience, kindness, goodness, faithfulness, gentleness, and self-control. Against such things there is no law." (Galatians 5:22-23)

- In Galatians 5:22-23, why are "love, joy, peace, patience, kindness, goodness, faithfulness, gentleness, and self-control" described as fruit?

Loving Others

- Explain the meaning of "against such things there is no law" in Galatians 5:22-23.

Listen, surrender, and trust

To live the graceful life, we are radically dependent on listening to, surrendering to, and trusting in the Holy Spirit. This is a moment-by-moment choice. Our problem is not lack of wisdom; it is lack of trust. We hear but we do not listen. We know but we do not believe. Surrender frightens us because it means giving up control.

- What are you trying to control instead of surrendering control to God?

We are not as powerful as we think we are when it comes to working out our lives. Much of what happens is beyond our control. While we always have a choice about how to respond in a given situation, we cannot control external circumstances.

- Give an example of an area in your life where you need to trust in God's plan.

Calling on the power of the Holy Spirit helps you administer grace. An "I can do it myself" determination changes to a prayer—"I cannot do it alone, please help." This helps you move into a more loving way of behaving.

- According to Philippians 2:13, where does authentic power come from?

God gives you "the power to do what pleases him," according to Philippians. (Philippians 2:13 NLT)

"For it is God who works in you to will and to act according to his good purpose." (Philippians 2:13)

- What are some of your temptations?

Relationships of Grace Workbook

- List three things that cause you to feel stress, worry, anger, sadness, or any other type of emotional turmoil.

Proverbs says, "Listen for God's voice in everything you do, everywhere you go." (Proverbs 3:6 MSG)

"Trust in the Lord with all your heart and lean not on your own understanding; in all your ways acknowledge him, and he will make your paths straight." (Proverbs 3:5-6)

- According to Proverbs 3:6 what should you do when you are faced with temptation and emotional turmoil?

Choose peace and fairness

Choice is key. The Holy Spirit guides you and works within to effect change. Your part is to make the right choices and trust in the power and wisdom of the Holy Spirit to help you do what is right.

- List three issues or decisions you are struggling with.

– Choose what you perceive to be the best options in dealing with these issues. It's not always easy to know if your choices are consistent with the guidance of the Holy Spirit. The Holy Spirit guides you to choose peace and fairness; you will be able to answer *yes* to all of the following questions if the Holy Spirit is providing the guidance. Considering your choices, answer the questions below.

- Are your choices consistent with God's Word? Are they consistent with love and God's commandments?

Because God works within you through the Holy Spirit, guidance will be consistent with Scripture. This is the greatest test of all.

70

Loving Others

- Are you comfortable with your choices?

Unhealthy choices create discomfort. Pay attention to inner turmoil. The right choices are sometimes uncomfortable, but you should feel a quiet conviction about your choices, even during times of conflict.

- Do your choices lead toward peace?

The Holy Spirit guides you toward peace, kindness, love, and conflict resolution. Choices are based in love, not fear.

- Do your choices account for the best interest of everyone involved?

The Holy Spirit will guide you to be kind but firm, and choose what is right. The Holy Spirit will not guide you in a manner that is self-destructive or insensitive toward others.

- Are the consequences fair?

Consequences are not always pleasant, but they should be just.

Theologian John Wesley said, "Do not hastily ascribe all things to God. Do not easily suppose dreams, voices, impressions, visions, or revelations to be from God. They may be from Him, they may be from nature, they may be from the devil."

Loving Others

The Golden Rule

The Rule

- Without using "do to" or "do unto," paraphrase the Golden Rule. (Matthew 7:12)

"Do to others what you would have them do to you." (Matthew 7:12)

- Explain how Jesus links the Golden Rule to the radical concept of loving your enemies in Luke 6:27-31.

- How are you being challenged to love your enemies?

"But I tell you who hear me: Love your enemies, do good to those who hate you, bless those who curse you, pray for those who mistreat you. If someone strikes you on one cheek, turn to him the other also. If someone takes your cloak, do not stop him from taking your tunic. Give to everyone who asks you, and if anyone takes what belongs to you, do not demand it back. Do to others as you would have them do to you." (Luke 6:27-31)

Karma or Grace?

Some compare karma to the Golden Rule, but they are not the same.

Karma is both your actions and the consequences of your actions in the form of an energy force. According to the principle of karma, your actions create a flow of energy that comes back to you in similar karma.

In Hinduism and Buddhism, the belief is karma creates ethical consequences that determine your destiny in your next life when you are reincarnated. The effects of karma accumulate

Relationships of Grace Workbook

over time. The goal is enlightenment—transcending karma by freeing yourself from negative karma through personal choice. Proper thoughts and actions enable you to reach a state of nirvana in Buddhism or *moksha* in Hinduism. According to the Hindu and Buddhist belief, this puts an end to your suffering and brings you freedom from reincarnation's cycle of death and rebirth.

The Christian belief is that salvation is through faith by grace. We will never be able to "achieve" enlightenment no matter how hard we try, and that is precisely why we need grace. God's grace is given freely as a gift; it is not earned through works. Consequences and reaping what you sow are consistent with Christian teachings, but for the ultimate purpose of bringing a person closer to God, not to balance a karmic scorecard.

"A man reaps what he sows." (Galatians 6:7)

- What did Paul teach in Galatians 6:7?

- Explain how consequences help you learn and grow closer to God.

"For it is by grace you have been saved, through faith--and this not from yourselves, it is the gift of God-- not by works, so that no one can boast." (Ephesians 2:8-9)

- Explain how grace is a gift of unconditional love according to Ephesians 2:8-9.

Grace offers the hope of undeserved mercy and unmerited favor. Through grace, we receive extravagant blessings we do not deserve and infinitely more blessings than we give. The scorecard never balances.

Golden Living

Ben Franklin said, "When you are good to others, you are best to yourself."

Living the Golden Rule is more than an obligatory moral response. It is what your heart longs to do. The Golden Rule is

Loving Others

more than a behavioral guide. It is an appeal for you to be yourself, a person created to love and be loved. In the graceful life, you are transformed from the inside out. You are motivated to do the right thing simply because it is the right thing to do.

- Thomas Aquinas, philosopher and theologian of the thirteenth century, said, "Sin is not disobedience of irrational authority, but the violation of human well-being." What does this mean?

Develop a heart for God

- In Matthew 22:36-40, why did Jesus teach the first and greatest commandment is to "love the Lord your God with all your heart and with all your soul and with all your mind"?

- What are some of the consequences of not loving God?

- What are the odds you will be able to "love your neighbor as yourself" if you don't put God first?

- What does the Great Commandment to "love your neighbor as yourself" teach you about loving yourself?

- Explain why setting boundaries are an essential aspect of keeping the Great Commandment in Matthew 22:36–40.

" 'Teacher, which is the greatest commandment in the Law?' Jesus replied, " 'Love the Lord your God with all your heart and with all your soul and with all your mind.' This is the first and greatest commandment. And the second is like it: 'Love your neighbor as yourself.' All the Law and the Prophets hang on these two commandments." (Matthew 22:36-40)

The Ten Commandments:

"You shall have no other gods before me.

"You shall not make for yourself an idol in the form of anything in heaven above or on the earth beneath or in the waters below. You shall not bow down to them or worship them; for I, the LORD your God, am a jealous God, punishing the children for the sin of the fathers to the third and fourth generation of those who hate me, but showing love to a thousand {generations} of those who love me and keep my commandments.

"You shall not misuse the name of the LORD your God, for the LORD will not hold

Relationships of Grace Workbook

anyone guiltless who misuses his name.

"Remember the Sabbath day by keeping it holy. Six days you shall labor and do all your work, but the seventh day is a Sabbath to the LORD your God. On it you shall not do any work, neither you, nor your son or daughter, nor your manservant or maidservant, nor your animals, nor the alien within your gates. For in six days the LORD made the heavens and the earth, the sea, and all that is in them, but he rested on the seventh day. Therefore the LORD blessed the Sabbath day and made it holy.

"Honor your father and your mother, so that you may live long in the land the LORD your God is giving you.

"You shall not murder.

"You shall not commit adultery.

"You shall not steal.

"You shall not give false testimony against your neighbor.

"You shall not covet your neighbor's house. You shall not covet your neighbor's wife, or his manservant or maidservant, his ox or donkey, or anything that belongs to your neighbor." (Exodus 20:3-17)

- What limits could you set that would help you follow the Great Commandment?

- Read the Ten Commandments in Exodus 20. It has been said if you live by the first two commandments, you will follow the other eight. What does this mean?

The commandment to love God is not for God's sake; it is for ours. When we love God, we experience a transformation of the heart. Only with a changed heart, one that has been molded for God, do we have any hope for loving others.

The Golden Rule calls us to consider the impact of our behavior on other people. I cannot do this on my own, but if I seek that which is greater than me, God will help. Self-responsibility is important, but I am not the only one at work.

Grace allows you to rest a little if you lean on God. When you ask Him to help, God will give you the grace you need.

- Give three examples from the last 24 hours of how seeking God in ordinary daily events and interactions with other people would have helped you live the Golden Rule.

Graceful living involves seeking God everywhere—in ordinary daily events, in our interactions with other people, and during times of conflict. Our only hope of loving our neighbors as ourselves is to receive God's grace and allow His grace to flow through us to other people.

Receiving grace is a choice that must be made from moment

Loving Others

to moment.

Give what you want to receive

Two words summarize the Golden Rule: give grace. God is the source of grace. But we become vessels of grace when we choose to open our hearts to it.

Become cognizant of the choices you make. Every encounter is an opportunity to administer grace.

The amount of love in your life is dependent on you, not other people. If you want more love in your life, act more lovingly. If you want to be treated with kindness and compassion, treat others with kindness and compassion. If you want others to accept you as you are, accept them as they are. If you want to be fed, feed the hungry.

- How can you bring more love into your life?

Living the Golden Rule is easier said than done. It calls you to forgive the unforgivable, love the unlovable, and be gracious to the graceless.

- Cite a recurring conflict and explain how you can respond by setting limits—kindly, with dignity and grace.

- While reflecting on a situation in which you experience emotional turmoil, explain how you can refrain from returning "evil for evil."

Loving Others

Acceptance

Disunity

Accepting people as they are is easy—as long as no people are involved.

The fundamental problem of not accepting people as they are is disunity. We experience hostility, judgment, and fear. We bicker and seek control. Disunity brings us out of relationship with one another. It makes it impossible to "love our neighbor as ourselves."

- Describe the challenge to which we are called according to 1 John 4:20–21.

Acceptance is . . .

Acceptance is the ability to choose peace regardless of external circumstances.

The benefits of acceptance are harmony, peace, and joy. Before we can love one another we have to accept one another. We don't all share a common viewpoint, but we can all share a common grace.

- List the benefits of accepting people as they are.

Acceptance is not . . .

Acceptance is not overlooking the truth or denying reality. It is not the same thing as agreeing with or condoning. Nor does acceptance mean you never set limits. It does not mean you become a doormat or tolerate abusive behavior. Set limits, work issues, negotiate as needed, but with a kind and accepting heart.

"If anyone says, 'I love God,' yet hates his brother, he is a liar. For anyone who does not love his brother, whom he has seen, cannot love God, whom he has not seen. And he has given us this command: Whoever loves God must also love his brother." (1 John 4:20–21)

Relationships of Grace Workbook

- Explain why limits are important when accepting a person as he or she is.

Don't overextend your reach

We reach too far when we try to change other people instead of accepting them as they are. If I extend my arm and move it in a circle around my head, the circle surrounds the only person I have the ability to change: me. I have no power to change anyone else.

- Who is the only person you have the ability to change?

One of the most powerful ways to effect change is to change ourselves. Giving up the fight to control others frees us to determine our own response. The focus shifts from trying to change the other person to looking at self.

- What is one of the most powerful ways to effect change?

Become a vessel of grace

One of the best parts about the graceful life is realizing I am far from perfect, but God loves me anyway. Who am I to not extend the same privilege of imperfection to others? When I become a vessel for grace, I allow the gift of unmerited favor and forgiveness I receive to flow through me to others.

- Share your thoughts about the following sentence: I am grateful God loves me in spite of my imperfections.

"Finally, all of you, live in harmony with one another; be sympathetic, love as brothers, be compassionate and humble. Do not repay evil with evil or insult with insult, but with blessing, because to this you were called so that you may inherit a blessing." (1 Peter 3: 8-9)

Other people have their own issues with which they are struggling. The less a person loves himself, the less love he will be able to offer you. How eloquently the New Testament teaches us to give grace anyway.

- According to 1 Peter 3:8-9, "God wants us to live in _____ with one another."

Loving Others

- How you can become a vessel of grace and extend grace to others? Be specific.

Defer to the Supreme Avenger

- In Deuteronomy 32:35, to whom does *mine* and *I* refer?

- According to Deuteronomy 32:36, who is on call for justice?

"It is mine to avenge; I will repay. In due time their foot will slip; their day of disaster is near and their doom rushes upon them." (Deuteronomy 32:35)

"The Lord will judge his people and have compassion on his servants when he sees their strength is gone and no one is left, slave or free." (Deuteronomy 32:36)

Look within

Fear-based emotions keep us from loving and accepting others.

Our ability to accept others is closely tied to our own self-esteem. When we love ourselves, it is easier to accept people as they are. When we feel inferior, acceptance is difficult.

What bothers us about someone else is often the same quality we see in ourselves. We notice the flaw because we are so familiar with it. The advice we give to others might be what we need to hear. We might be embarrassed by a family member's weakness and view it as a negative reflection on ourselves.

– Answer the following questions keeping those you are having trouble accepting in mind.

- What about *me* is inhibiting acceptance?

- Am I expecting another person to validate me instead of accepting God's love?

Relationships of Grace Workbook

- Do I have the quality I am viewing as a flaw in someone else?

- Am I struggling with self-love?

- How am I struggling for control?

- Am I struggling to belong?

- Is my motive self-seeking?

- Do I want the other person to change to help me look or feel better?

- Have I acknowledged that the other person has his own issues? Am I allowing grace to flow through me anyway?

- Do I seek peace or do I want to mold the perfect person?

CHAPTER FOUR

Living with Meaning

Have you ever asked yourself any of the questions below?

– Why am I here?

– Is this all there is?

– What is my purpose in life?

– How can I experience passion?

– What is the meaning of life?

If so, you, like many people, have been challenged to understand how you can live with a sense of meaning and purpose.

Survival Through Meaning

• Referring to the "Survival Through Meaning" section of *Relationships of Grace,* what gave Frankl the will to survive?

Meaning enters our lives through our relationships and by living in accordance with God's plan. You do not "find" your purpose through goal setting and achievement, although proper planning and preparation are important. Your purpose unfolds as you seek to understand God's desires for you and trust Him to help you follow His will.

• How does meaning enter our lives?

Relationships of Grace Workbook

- Why do many goal-setting exercises not reveal your purpose in life? What is the missing link?

You were born with talents, given to you as a gift of grace, to be used in a way to help others. Passion, purpose, and meaning are the by-product of living in accordance with the divine plan for your life.

- According to Scott Peck in *The Road Less Traveled*, how can you understand the significance of your life?

In *The Road Less Traveled,* Scott Peck wrote, "Once we perceive the reality of grace, our understanding of ourselves as meaningless and insignificant is shattered."

- Why?

We'll explore living with meaning further as we discuss:

- Passion

- Making a Difference

- Freedom from Illusions

- Dreams Come True

- Joy in the Journey

- Foot Washing for Grace

Passion

Clinging to Our Rafts

At the beginning of the "Passion" section in *Relationships of Grace,* I told the story of clinging to a raft with five other rafters as rapids crashed upon our heads. We gripped so tightly that, when the raft flipped, we were thrown beneath it in the churning, forty-three degree whitewater. We feared leaving the comfort and security of our raft so much that we found ourselves trapped underwater. We felt safe right up until the raft flipped.

The fear of leaving our comfort zone keeps us from living our passion. Venturing away from the raft is risky.

- What is your raft? Is there something you are clinging to as the waves crash upon your head? Are you hanging on to an unhealthy relationship because you are afraid to be alone? Are you settling for a job you hate because it pays well? Do you face daily boredom because you are afraid to leave the security of your comfort zone?

- Are you not pursuing something you feel called to do because you are afraid to risk venturing away from your raft? Explain.

- If you were to create a "regret minimization framework" as Jeff Bezos did, what would it look like?

Before Jeff Bezos founded Amazon.com, he created what he calls a "regret minimization framework." He pictured himself as an eighty-year-old man looking back on his life with as few regrets as possible. Bezos reasoned he would not regret trying and failing, but would regret never having tried. Bezos left his job on Wall Street to follow his dream. Amazon.com was born.

Life-Giving Benefits

- Why do you believe people like Jeff Bezos and Bill Gates keep working when they could afford to quit?

Thomas Jefferson died on July 4, 1826, exactly fifty years after he signed the Declaration of Independence. Jefferson spoke his last words on the evening of July 3, "Is it July fourth yet?" He wasn't going anywhere until he celebrated the fiftieth anniversary of his passion.

The line between work and play is blurred when you pursue your passion. A job does not feel like work when you love it. It's fun. At the end of the week you may even feel a twinge of sorrow because the workweek is over.

Pursuing your passion is exhilarating. It transports you into a new and exciting world.

Passion is energizing. We describe passionate people as being "full of life." Apathy drains life.

Unveil your graceful gifts

When a daffodil bulb is planted, the bulb's mission is to produce a daffodil, not a tulip. If the bulb devoted its energy to trying to become a tulip, it would never succeed. Nor would it realize its natural beauty as a daffodil.

You were born with incredible gifts. These gifts are yours to contribute to humanity.

Here's the best part. Whatever your special gifts are, you love to use them! When you are doing what you are born to do, you experience a deep sense of joy, fulfillment, and meaning.

The book of Romans teaches, "We have different gifts, according to the grace given us." (Romans 12:6)

- What does Romans 12:6 teach?

We are all born with different gifts. Some are called to enforce the law, others to teach the law. Some are visionaries of the big picture; others are masterful at carrying out the details.

- Where do your gifts come from according to Romans 12:3-6?

"It's important that you not misinterpret yourselves as people who are bringing this goodness to God. No. God brings it all to you. The only accurate way to understand ourselves is by what God is and by what he does for us, not by

By understanding your talents are gifts from God, you will view your gifts humbly. Instead of feeling pride, you will experience gratitude. You will become less envious of others because you will view their talents in terms of who they were

Living with Meaning

created to be rather than associating gifts with a person's value as a human being.

- List 20 talents or positive qualities you have been given. I encourage you to continue writing until you have written a minimum of 20. Place an asterisk by those you feel most passionate about.

what we are and what we do for him. . . Let's just go ahead and be what we were made to be, without enviously or pridefully comparing ourselves with each other, or trying to be something we aren't." (Romans 12:3-6 MSG)

- How can you use your gifts to help others?

Surrender to the divine plan

Finding your passion is like breathing. You *have* to do it.

Relationships of Grace Workbook

People have commented about how disciplined I must be to write a book. True, writing requires discipline, but love motivates me more than discipline. Why wouldn't I want to do something I love?

Risk is one reason we can be reticent. Discovering passion requires us to risk leaving the security of our comfort zone. If I had not chosen to leave a lucrative twenty-year career in computer software engineering, my dream would be burning within me.

- Is fear keeping you from risking and leaving the security of your comfort zone to live your passion?

- How might your comfort zone not be as secure as you would like to believe?

"For I know the plans I have for you," declares the Lord, "plans to prosper you and not to harm you, plans to give you hope and a future." (Jeremiah 29:11)

The only real security is in God.

Finding purpose is about surrendering, not searching, and using the gifts given to you. Living God's plan is how a daffodil bulb grows into a daffodil and not a tulip.

- According to Jeremiah 29:11, your life is not haphazard, unplanned, or unintentional. Fill in the blank: There is a divine _____ for your life.

- Put your name in the blank from the following passage from Jeremiah 29:11.

- "For I know the plans I have for you, _____," declares the Lord, "plans to prosper you and not to harm you, plans to give you hope and a future." (Jeremiah 29:11)

"Trust in the Lord with all thine heart; and lean not unto thine own understanding. In all thy ways acknowledge Him, and He shall direct thy paths." (Proverbs 3:5–6)

- Proverbs 3:5–6 is the how-to of finding your passion. Paraphrase it.

Living with Meaning

God will give you the grace you need to live in accordance with His plans for you. And you will be richly rewarded as you live passionately with a sense of meaning and purpose.

Plan and prepare

Opportunity is lost without planning and preparation. If I am going in for surgery, I prefer the person holding the knife to be someone who is trained in surgery. It goes without saying it takes time to plan and prepare for your life's mission.

Living with purpose does not mean you abdicate your responsibilities or abandon your family in pursuit of passion. Priorities change over time, depending on family and personal needs. Life balance includes integrating passion and responsibilities as you love and serve the world around you.

- How might you plan and prepare to pursue your passion?

Living with Meaning

Making a Difference

Making a Difference

You can make an impact in the lives of those around you by infusing love into your daily work. Whatever the task, you can make it meaningful.

Work does not mean you are getting paid in a job outside your home. Raising young children and volunteering in your community is meaningful work. The key is you are engaged in productive activities and adding value to the world around you.

You have the opportunity to make a difference in the world every day.

The difference between a meaningful and meaningless job is often perception, or attitude. Living with a sense of significance can be as simple as changing your perspective. A determination to make an impact and to help others as you perform your daily duties may be all you need to enrich your life and the lives of those around you.

Meaningless Consequences

The human brain wants to be stimulated. The heart wants to serve.

Without a sense of purpose and meaning, we lose our passion for life. Days are long and unfulfilling. Apathy, frustration, boredom, fear, feeling incapable, envy, and depression are some of the consequences of living without a sense of meaning.

Understand the mission

- 1 Corinthians 12:4-7 names three things "there are different kinds of." What are they?

"There are different kinds of gifts, but the same Spirit. There are different kinds of service, but the same Lord. There are different kinds of working, but the same God works all of them in all men. Now to each one the manifestation of the Spirit is given for the common good." (1 Corinthians 12:4-7)

Relationships of Grace Workbook

- According to 1 Corinthians 12:4-7, the "manifestation of the Spirit" is given for what purpose?

Understand how the work being performed contributes to humanity. This involves seeing past the immediate task. A mother sees above the pile of dirty laundry to her angel in diapers. A teacher sees past Tuesday's math assignment and remembers she is helping to shape the next generation. A bus driver caught among honking horns in traffic understands mass transit is important for a healthier environment and knows he is helping those unable to afford a car. The garbage collector remembers when the city of New York was paralyzed without his services.

- Reflecting on the "bigger picture," how does your work contribute to humanity?

Be creative

Adding value, being creative, and producing reaps fulfillment.

- When do you feel the most energized and fulfilled?

Minister

Preachers are not the only people who are called to minister. We all are.

Mother Teresa did not stride onto the world stage as the saint she later became. She stepped into one small corner of a broken world and held the hand of an ailing person. After caring for that person, she moved on to the next.

"It is not what we do but how much love we put into it," Mother Teresa said. She told some people who went to help in

92

Living with Meaning

Calcutta to find their own Calcutta. You don't need to move to the slums of India to make a difference. Find your own small corner of the world and minister.

You are surrounded daily by broken spirits. Those who are not shattered are so fragile they need daily doses of love.

To minister is to serve. The greatest hindrance to serving others is self-absorption. It's tough to give without some expectation of getting.

The secret to overcoming this paradigm is revealed in *Practicing the Presence of God*, written by Brother Lawrence, a seventeenth century monk—*whatever you do, do it for God.* When you buy a gift, fix dinner for a sick neighbor, complete a project at work, take a walk in the park, or call a loved one—do it for God. To paraphrase Mother Teresa, it's not between you and the other person, it's between you and God.

–   Fill in the blanks below with three ways you plan on serving this week.

•   I am going to _____
    for God.

•   I am going to _____
    for God.

•   I am going to _____
    for God.

•   According to 1 Peter 4:10, what is the primary purpose of your gifts?

•   How can you use your gifts to minister to others in your normal, daily routine?

"Each one should use whatever gift he has received to serve others, faithfully administering God's grace in its various forms." (1 Peter 4:10)

Your experiences, especially your trials, help you develop your gifts. Meaning is found in suffering when you grow through your trials and use your experiences to love and serve the world around you. The best teachers are those who have experienced the troubles of their students.

God wants you to use your pain for the greater good.

Relationships of Grace Workbook

In *The Purpose Driven Life,* Rick Warren writes, "Your *greatest* ministry will most likely come out of your greatest hurt . . . God intentionally allows you to go through painful experiences to equip you for ministry to others."

- What are your greatest hurts?

God "comforts us in all our troubles, so that we can comfort those in any trouble with the comfort we ourselves have received from God." (2 Corinthians 1:4)

- How does God help you use your suffering to help others according to 2 Corinthians 1:4?

"He comes alongside us when we go through hard times, and before you know it, he brings us alongside someone else who is going through hard times so that we can be there for that person just as God was there for us." (2 Corinthians 1:4 MSG)

- How might you use your pain and learning experiences to help others?

You can make a difference. The opportunity is present for everyone, whether you are a carpool driver, a CEO, a member of the PTA, or working in a nine-to-five job.

You were created with special gifts to "serve others, faithfully administering God's grace in its various forms." (1 Peter 4:10)

Living with Meaning

Freedom from Illusions

Relationships of Grace tells the story of the emperor of an ancient dynasty who commissioned the Terracotta Warriors and an underground tomb to keep evil spirits away and protect his soul in the after life. Seven thousand life-sized soldiers, horses, and chariots are housed in an underground palace. Each warrior has a different expression. Each was given an authentic weapon. All face east in the direction of the emperor's enemies. Some are archers; others are soldiers, generals, or officers. A power structure exists even in clay armies.

Material World

It's difficult to understand the logic of a man so powerful and wealthy he created an underground palace in the hope of eternal rest after death. Most people in modern-day society understand the emperor's hopes were an illusion.

- What parallels can be drawn about the emperor and people in modern-day society?

- What parallels can be drawn about the emperor and you?

Our egos coax us to project a certain type of image and chase money, power, status, and achievement. Our egos entice us to strive to be the best, achieve more, accumulate wealth and

95

Relationships of Grace Workbook

possessions, and receive the next promotion even if it's in a job we hate.

But prizes of the ego can be a burden.

- How does your ego entice you to project a certain type of image or chase material goals at the expense of spiritual ones?

A material approach enslaves us to things and achievements. Money, power, status, and achievement are seductive, but they will never fill a spiritual void. Nothing is inherently wrong with buying nice things. I would rather have money than not any day. The problem is when we are driven by external rewards at the expense of a life outside of grace.

- How do you strive to satisfy your need for love and security by pursuing money, power, status, and achievement instead of allowing yourself to be drawn into grace?

- Prioritize the following list according to your value system, with *1* being your highest priority and *7* being your lowest priority.

_____ God
_____ Worldly power
_____ Family
_____ Achievement
_____ Money
_____ Status
_____ Friends

- Rank the following list according to how you spend your time and energy, with *1* being the area you devote the most time and energy to and *7* the least.

_____ God
_____ Worldly power
_____ Family
_____ Achievement
_____ Money
_____ Status
_____ Friends

- Comparing the two lists, are your priorities consistent with how you spend your time and energy? Explain.

Living with Meaning

- Referring to Proverbs 13:7, which best characterizes your life?

_____ Pretentious, showy, and empty
_____ Plain, simple, and full life
_____ A combination of both of the above

Proverbs teaches, "A pretentious, showy life is an empty life; a plain and simple life is a full life." (Proverbs 13:7)

Non-Material Benefits

Meaning is not material. Meaning enters our lives through our relationships and by living into God's plan by using the gifts given to us, in grace, to love and serve humanity.

In moments when you allow yourself to be drawn into grace, you are freed from the burden of the ego's illusions. Life is enriched with meaning, joy, and passion. Your relationships improve. Gratitude for what you have replaces an insatiable longing for what you do not have. Serenity replaces a continual striving for more. Work energizes rather than drains you. Creativity soars.

Move from having to being

You cannot experience the fullness of life through achievement. Buying, searching, and striving keep you from life in the spirit.

Mystic Meister Eckhart taught, to become more spiritual, we must transcend the ego.

The first Beatitude teaches the first step into the graceful life and reveals the path to the full life of Proverbs 13:7.

- What is the first Beatitude? Refer to Matthew 5:3.

"Blessed are the poor in spirit, for theirs is the kingdom of heaven." (Matthew 5:3)

"You're blessed when you're at the end of your rope. With less of you there is more of God and his rope." (Matthew 5:3 MSG)

- According to the translation of the first Beatitude in Matthew 5:3 NLT, what does God want you to realize?

"God blesses those who realize their need for him, for the Kingdom of Heaven is given to them." (Matthew 5:3 NLT)

- Strongholds and longings for unmet expectations keep you in emotional turmoil, precluding life in the spirit. Describe some of your strongholds and unmet expectations.

Relationships of Grace Workbook

- How does the desire to prove you are right keep you from being in the spirit?

- How does striving for money, power, status, and achievement keep you from being poor in spirit?

Abstract absolutes do not define the doorway into the blessed life of the first Beatitude. Annual income and the number of awards hanging on the wall do not separate the rich from the poor in spirit. The heart does. Self-sufficiency, lack of trust, and strongholds that separate you from God keep you from God's kingdom.

Blessed are those who allow themselves to be drawn into and immersed in grace, moment by moment.

Simplify

"Jesus looked around and said to his disciples, 'How hard it is for the rich to enter the kingdom of God.'" (Mark 10:23)

"24 Seeing his reaction, Jesus said, 'Do you have any idea how difficult it is for people who have it all to enter God's kingdom? 25 I'd say it's easier to thread a camel through a needle's eye than get a rich person into God's kingdom.' 26 'Then who has any chance at all?' the others asked. 27 'No chance at all,' Jesus said, 'if you think you can pull it off by yourself. Every chance in the world if you trust God to do it.'" (Luke 18: 24-27 MSG)

The concept of simplicity is simple. Simplicity is freedom from the bondage of things that are burdensome: compulsion for material goods, power, status, money, and achievement. It is a retreat from a hectic pace keeping us so busy we don't have time for that which is most important. Less becomes more. Simplicity begins with the understanding that wealth and the good life are lived in the spirit, not through the material world. It is acknowledging that every blessing is a gift of grace.

- In Mark 10:23, what did Jesus mean when he said it is hard "for the rich to enter the kingdom of God"?

- According to Luke 18:27 MSG, what is your chance of entering God's kingdom if you "think you can pull it off by yourself"?

- According to Luke 18:27 MSG, what must you do to enter God's kingdom?

Living with Meaning

Dreams Come True

Passion, Purpose, and Courage

Life is an exciting adventure when you live with passion and a sense of purpose. Your passion and dreams align with the divine plan for your life.

- What are your dreams?

The divine plan for your life is found amidst your dreams and passions.

Following your dreams takes courage. Courage is often misunderstood. Some people equate it with being fearless. But courageous people fear. They face difficult situations in spite of their fears.

- If you were to die tomorrow, would you have been living your dreams?

- Is something keeping you from following your dreams? If so, what?

Eleanor Roosevelt said, "You gain strength, courage, and confidence by every experience in which you really stop to look fear in the face. . . . You must do the thing you think you cannot do."

Relationships of Grace Workbook

Different Parts, Equal Value

No one prevails in the Tour de France without his team. Nine athletes are on each of the twenty-one competing teams. The teammates' job is to help the lead biker cross the finish line first.

Lance Armstrong graciously acknowledges the role his team plays in victory. The team brings Armstrong water when he is thirsty, feeds him when he is hungry, and shields him from the wind by riding at the front of the pack while Armstrong rides closely behind the team to save his energy. Near the finish line, the team moves aside and Armstrong breaks free to cross the line in victory.

The team is in the backdrop. I cannot tell you the name of one person on Armstrong's team. But the world knows the name Lance Armstrong.

The team makes the Tour possible. Imagine pedaling for 2,500 miles, your heart pounding so hard you feel nauseous, to help another guy cross the finish line first. Nine guys were on the U.S. team, but only one could finish first. The others served in the shadows of the winner's spotlight. Every teammate was critically important. The eight who followed are of equal value to the one who led. Without the team, there would be no Tour.

You were created to live with purpose and to pursue your part on the team. Each role is different, all of equal value.

- What is the caution of Romans 12:3? Answer by giving an example.

"Do not think of yourself more highly than you ought, but rather think of yourself with sober judgment, in accordance with the measure of faith God has given you. Just as each of us has one body with many members, and these members do not all have the same function, so in Christ we who are many form one body, and each member belongs to all the others. We have different gifts, according to the grace given us." (Romans 12:3-6)

- According to Romans 12:3-6, where do your gifts come from?

- What role, or mission, were you created for? If you are not sure, brainstorm by writing down your strengths and the things you love to do.

100

Living with Meaning

Embrace the uncertainty of the graceful path

Passion is experienced through the unknown.

Living with passion often brings you face to face with the uncertainty of new experiences. Uncertainty is not the same thing as impossibility. Taking on a challenge with an unknown outcome such as a new project, changing jobs, making new friends, traveling, or learning a new skill can be invigorating.

- What uncertainties are you afraid of?

- How do these unknowns keep you from taking the risks necessary to follow your dreams?

Following your dream is exhilarating. Situations you are anxious about are often also exciting. Part of accepting the uncertainty of the graceful path is to embrace the excitement of the unknown.

Believe

Belief is the cornerstone of realized dreams.

- Describe your beliefs.

For people who live their dreams, problems and shortcomings are challenges, not excuses for quitting. Believing includes surrendering by accepting God's will, having the faith to pursue the divine plan for your life, and trusting that God will be with you as you do.

God-confidence creates self-confidence.

Relationships of Grace Workbook

"May the God of hope fill you with all joy and peace as you trust in him, so that you may overflow with hope by the power of the Holy Spirit." (Romans 15:13)

- What are some of the benefits of trusting God according to Romans 15:13?

- How is fear keeping you from living God's plan for your life?

- How can you lower your level of anxiety and increase your trust in God? Be specific.

If you pursue your calling, and if it is God's plan for you, *it* will happen. *It* does not mean winning or achieving material gains. With perseverance and by putting your hand in God's, you will experience contentment as your dreams come true.

- Are you living God's plans for your life or struggling on your own? Elaborate.

- What spiritual disciplines can you incorporate into your daily life to help you trust in God and pursue your dreams?

Joy in the Journey

Blessings of "Un"

Some of life's greatest blessings are described with "un" adjectives. Unanticipated blessing. Unplanned good fortune. Unexpected gain. Unsolicited advantage. Unscheduled windfall. Unpredicted benefit. Unforeseen treasure.

The problem is we can become so focused on the outcome we miss the journey. Priorities get out of balance. External factors motivate us rather than our internal value system as we seek artificial rewards. When we become fixated on a particular path, we often miss the better way.

- What outcomes are you so absorbed with that you miss the joy in the journey?

How do you live in the present and enjoy the journey instead of being so driven toward a particular outcome? The secret lies in learning to trust in some different "un" words: uncertainty, unknown, unattached.

In the graceful life, you open yourself to risk the unknown, embrace uncertainty, and trust in the outcome *by living into the divine plan for your life*. You remain passionate and committed to the process, but unattached to a particular outcome.

- According Psalm 40:1-4a, when you are willing to be patient, what does the Lord do?

"[1] I waited patiently for the Lord; he turned to me and heard my cry.
[2] He lifted me out of the slimy pit, out of the mud and mire; he set my feet on a rock and gave me a firm place to stand.
[3] He put a new song in my mouth, a hymn of praise to our God. Many will see and fear and put their trust in the Lord.
[4] Blessed is the man who makes the Lord his trust." (Psalm 40:1-4a)

Relationships of Grace Workbook

- In Psalm 40: 2, who is doing the lifting? What does this verse teach you about self-sufficiency?

Your calling is often found amid uncertainty. As you make choices to align your will with divine will, you will experience a joyful journey rich in blessings more extravagant than you can imagine.

All because of one other "un" word: unfailing love.

- What is the promise of Psalm 40:4 if you trust in the Lord?

"Blessed are you who give yourselves over to God, turn your backs on the world's 'sure thing,' ignore what the world worships." (Psalm 40:4 MSG)

Watch for providential paths

Relationships of Grace tells the story of Oprah's "lucky break" and some divine incidents.

- What are some experiences you have had that some might describe as coincidences, but you believe to be divine incidents?

An artist was heartbroken when her work was not selected for display at a prestigious art gallery in another state. Feeling rejected and depressed, she returned home. The following year she sold more than a million dollars worth of artwork in her home state.

- What incidents left you heartbroken, but later turned out to be blessings?

Living with Meaning

- What does Jeremiah 29:11 teach you about these incidents?

" 'For I know the plans I have for you', declares the Lord, 'plans to prosper you and not to harm you, plans to give you hope and a future.' " (Jeremiah 29:11)

In *Addiction and Grace,* Gerald May wrote, "Miracles are nothing other than God's ordinary truth seen through surprised eyes."

- What are some miracles you have witnessed?

God is always at work. The Spirit blows us like the wind. We never know which way the hand of God will lead us, only that the hand is always there. (John 3:8)

- Paraphrase John 3:8.

"You know well enough how the wind blows this way and that. You hear it rustling through the trees, but you have no idea where it comes from or where it's headed next. That's the way it is with everyone "born from above' by the wind of God, the Spirit of God." (John 3:8 MSG)

"The wind blows wherever it pleases. You hear its sound, but you cannot tell where it comes from or where it is going. So it is with everyone born of the Spirit." (John 3:8)

- Citing a specific example from your own life, explain why you can never be certain about the outcome according to John 3:8.

As you allow yourself to be drawn into grace, you open yourself to exploring the providential paths of divine planning.

Focus on the journey, not the outcome

- When have you been so focused on the outcome you missed the journey?

Relationships of Grace Workbook

- Are you missing the journey today?

Outcome-oriented goals categorize results into win/lose dichotomies. Goals are useful to the extent they provide a plan for moving in a certain direction. The problem is when emotional energy and feelings of self-worth are tied to a specific result over which you have no control.

To paraphrase the popular expression "success is a journey, not a destination," focus on the journey, not the outcome. The joy is in the journey, not the achievement.

This means, in school, the focus is on learning rather than grades. At work, the emphasis is on doing a quality job, enjoying your work, and being kind to your coworkers rather than the next promotion. Driving includes enjoying the scenery along the way. Parents' emphasis is on loving their children and spending time together instead of raising the best athlete or the class valedictorian.

- Write three specific ways you can enjoy the journey more and be less anxious about the outcome.

Life is a growth-process. Nobody masters life. Yes, plan and prepare, but who knows what curves the future will bring?

You choose your attitude and actions, but are powerless over most outcomes.

Focus on the journey, not the outcome. Travel down providential paths. Experience the joy in the journey.

Living with Meaning

Foot Washing for Grace

The world stands in awe of a small but powerful woman. She wore no makeup and dressed in sandals and a sari. Her image was different than the airbrushed models on the covers of women's magazines. She did not live in a mansion on the hill. Her home was in the slums.

Mother Teresa devoted her life to serving the poor on the streets of Calcutta. She was living proof of the power of love. Her life was service in action and as close as humans get to agape—perfect, other-centered love. She was selflessly devoted to the welfare of others.

India honored her with a funeral of the state, even though she was a Christian in a Hindu country. Agape love spans religious boundaries.

- How do you suppose Mother Teresa was able to transcend differences in religious and cultural beliefs?

Riches to Rags to Blessings

- What does Matthew 22:39 teach about serving others?

"And the second is like it: 'Love your neighbor as yourself.'" (Matthew 22:39)

Psychologist Abraham Maslow performed a study of happy people. He found when a person is "radiantly alive," he is living for a purpose "beyond himself."

You have been created with such magnificence that when you spotlight grace by serving others, the light bounces back to you. When you serve others, your own life is enriched.

Winston Churchill said, "We make a living by what we get. We make a life by what we give."

- Explain how your life been enriched by serving others.

- When have you given to others and felt like you got back more than you gave?

Mother Teresa defined love as "giving until it hurts."

- Why is it so difficult for us to share the unconditional love God affords us?

- Why are you more likely to give to others when you trust God?

"Jesus replied: 'Love the Lord your God with all your heart and with all your soul and with all your mind.' This is the first and greatest commandment." (Matthew 22:37-38)

- How does honoring the Great Commandment (Matthew 22:37-38) make you more likely to serve others?

Service is love in action. Every act of service, no matter how small, puts more love into the world.

Service is any act of kindness that is performed in the best interest of another person. This does not mean you do everything for another person. For example, it is often more appropriate for parents to train their children so they learn how to carry their own load. If parents carry their children's burdens for them, their help can hurt.

- What is an example of carrying another person's burden instead of setting limits?

Living with Meaning

Dirty Feet Scrubbed Clean

Washing a guest's feet was an act of hospitality in Biblical times. During the Passover Feast, Jesus picked up a towel, filled a bowl with water, and washed the feet of his disciples—even Judas. The same hands that would have nails driven through them washed the feet of the one who was to betray him.

Humility is an integral part of service

In Biblical times, people walked around barefoot, or in sandals at best. Bathing was done infrequently in the local river, and without soap.

Only the slaves performed such a mundane and disagreeable task such as washing another person's feet. And yet Jesus humbled himself in an act of total submission to teach the lesson of humility in service.

- What can we learn from Jesus example of washing the disciples' feet in John 13:4-5?

"He got up from the meal, took off his outer clothing, and wrapped a towel around his waist. After that, he poured water into a basin and began to wash his disciples' feet, drying them with the towel that was wrapped around him." (John 13:4-5)

Most acts of service are simple acts of kindness

You do not need to give up your house and live on the streets of Calcutta to serve. Most acts of service are not the extraordinary tasks we make them out to be. What is more menial than washing someone's grimy feet?

The director of the local food bank told me most of their food donations come from people in less affluent neighborhoods. The poor know what it is like to be hungry. Perhaps that explains part of the reason caring people of affluence can be reluctant to serve. They do not understand the difference a can of soup can make.

- Following Mother Teresa's teaching, list five simple ways you can serve "in small things with great love."

Mother Teresa taught we love "not in big things, but in small things with great love."

Service is anything that creates unity. To serve is to share some soup, aid the ailing, hammer nails for the homeless, invite the ignored, and give grace to the grouch. Many acts of service

Relationships of Grace Workbook

cost nothing and take little time: encouragement, compliments, listening, gratitude, and compassion. Anytime you affirm the worth of others, you serve.

– Give a specific example of how you can serve through:

• Encouragement

• Compliments

• Listening

• Gratitude

• Compassion

Service is other-centered, not self-serving

Jesus washed the disciples' feet in the anonymity of an upper room. No audience. No fans. Just some grimy feet and a washbowl. Only the men, whose feet he knelt before, were present. Jesus received no adulation from a crowd, no personal glorification.

He taught by example: Perform menial tasks with humility and be other-centered, not self-serving.

• Compare and contrast self-serving service versus service done in the anonymity of an upper room.

CHAPTER FIVE

The Spiritual Journey

The Sanctuary Within

Spirituality is not just for monks. We all yearn for spiritual fulfillment, including people who live normal lives raising children and going to work every day.

Drawing closer to God and becoming more spiritually centered helps you develop a reverence for life. Relationships improve. Worries lessen. Blessings are found in the mundane. Less becomes more. Strangers become friends.

When you nurture your spirituality, you journey to the sanctuary within, a place of inner retreat no one else can reach. You are freed to experience serenity among the chaos. This does not mean you never experience conflict, but when you do, inner tranquility helps you respond in grace.

Choosing the spiritual journey is a magnificent way to travel through a troubled world, living in the hope and safety of God's loving care.

Spirituality or Religion?

Laws cannot cure the broken spirits of evil acts. The heart must be changed.

Your heart is transformed as you allow yourself to be immersed in grace and develop a personal relationship with God. This helps you develop an awareness that blessings are from God. This is a process. Moment by moment, you are free to choose to love God, accept God's love for you, and administer grace to others. Sacred moments are those in which you relinquish self-sufficiency, recognize your dependence on, and trust in God. Instead of knowing *about* God, you know Him. These are blessed moments.

Spirituality is not the same as religion. It is not synonymous with going to church or understanding religious doctrine. Some spiritual people never go to church. Others who spend a lot of

111

Relationships of Grace Workbook

time in the pew on Sunday mornings spend little time in relationship with The One they come to worship. Personal relationship is the key.

We'll explore the spiritual journey as we discuss:

- Knowing God

- Centering Prayer

- Gratitude and Grace

- Solitude

The Spiritual Journey

Knowing God

Searching for Fullness

Too often, as we seek love, we ignore the Greatest Love of all. Our yearning for God is so fundamental to our existence that, by design, the yearning is never completely satisfied. The longing keeps us seeking and growing.

One of the things He wants most is our friendship. It is difficult to appreciate the magnificence of something so vast you can never fully understand it. The sacred landscape is too overwhelming, too grand, and too incomprehensible. A personal relationship with God frees you to live in hope and reach through the brokenness with healing hands to a world desperately in need of grace.

It is then that you learn how to love and be loved and to live with meaning.

Self, Self, and More Self

The I-do-it-myself syndrome keeps you from accepting the gift of God's grace.

– For each of the following scenarios, give an example of how you resort to self-sufficiency.

• Resort to self-mastery instead of surrendering to the Master.

• Run on willpower instead of resting in the Greater Power.

• Strive for your own will instead of accepting divine will.

- Fear the future instead of trusting in the Planner of the future.

- Seek control instead of seeking the Kingdom.

- Walk alone instead of leaning on God.

A Changed Heart

A changed heart changes your life. While we have the responsibility to make good choices, it takes the power of grace to change our hearts. Legalistic approaches and trying harder are never enough without internal, spiritual transformation.

- Referring to Psalm 51:10 and Proverbs 4:23, why did David ask for a clean heart?

"Create in me a clean heart, O God," David penned in the Psalm. (Psalm 51:10 AMP)

"Above all else, guard your heart, for it is the wellspring of life," according to Solomon's proverb. (Proverbs 4:23)

On the spiritual journey, your choice is whether or not to accept the gift of grace and enter into a personal relationship with God. When you accept the invitation, God does the work of changing your heart. He transforms you from the inside out.

- To be changed from the inside out, what choice to you have to make according to Romans 12:1-2?

The Apostle Paul said, "Embracing what God does for you is the best thing you can do for him . . . fix your attention on God. You'll be changed from the inside out." (Romans 12:1–2 MSG)

Fear of punishment does not change a heart of hatred to one of love. Spiritual transformation does.

Vessels of Grace

"Know God. Receive and reflect grace." Six words summarize the central message of *Relationships of Grace*.

Let God fill you with His Spirit; you will then become a vessel of grace.

- According to 2 Corinthians 3:3, how do you receive the "Spirit of the Living God"?

The "Spirit of the Living God" is written "not on tablets of stone but on tablets of human hearts," the Apostle Paul said. (2 Corinthians 3:3)

Inviting God into your life is a longing, not an obligation, a

The Spiritual Journey

joy not a burden. It is the only way to quench the thirst, the only way to heal the ache. In the Old Testament, God explains the commandments are "for your own good."

You are healed through the transforming love of God. As you are healed, the reverberating sounds of love begin to echo deep within, influencing your thoughts and actions.

- Read Deuteronomy 10:13 and complete the following sentence: Observing the commandments are for your own

  _____.

- What did Saint Augustine of Hippo mean when he said, "Love God and do as you please"?

"Observe the Lord's commands and decrees that I am giving you today for your own good." (Deuteronomy 10:13)

The self-sufficient try to propel themselves into goodness and happiness. But how good is good enough? If you focus on morality but neglect the importance of a personal relationship with God, you will never live in integrity. But when a relationship with God is maintained, morality follows.

The commandment in Deuteronomy 6:5 to "love the Lord your God with all your heart and with all your soul and with all your strength" is not an edict. It is an appeal to the heart.

Knowing Through Relationship

Western culture perpetuates the idea of an external God *out there* somewhere. The Bible teaches otherwise.

- What do Luke 17:21 and 1 John 4:4 teach?

"The kingdom of God is within you." (Luke 17:21)

"The one who is in you is greater than the one who is in the world." (1 John 4:4)

This does not mean we are little gods. God works within, but is also separate and distinct from us. God is greater. God is always more.

The spiritual journey is the process of moving deeper into the kingdom of God. The quest to find one's self is really a journey to find God.

God created us to be in relationship with Him. This means knowing God through relationship rather than knowledge. It means resting in His presence and communicating with Him moment to moment, throughout the day.

Legalism and works-oriented religion substitute rules, dogma, knowledge, and judgment at the expense of a personal relationship with God. It is not uncommon to become consumed with activities of religious institutional life and miss the joy, peace, and transformation of knowing God.

115

Relationships of Grace Workbook

" 'You will seek me and find me when you seek me with all your heart. I will be found by you,' declares the Lord, 'and will bring you back from captivity.' " (Jeremiah 29:13–14)

- According to Jeremiah 29:13–14, what must you do if you want to find God?

- When you earnestly seek God, what is the promise of Jeremiah 29:13–14?

Head to Heart

Faith, by definition, involves trust without proof. Mystery and paradox are an integral part of faith. God is the ultimate mystery—perhaps by design, because it keeps us seeking Him.

The mystery is not to be solved, but entered into.

We come to know God by experiencing God's presence.

I am humbled by the profound love of a deeply caring God whose infinite love is too vast to be understood by the limitations of my human mind.

- Write a brief account of your faith journey.

Ask, seek, and knock

The first step on the spiritual journey is to acknowledge our need for help. This is more than a casual request. It is a plea for mercy. It is the humble acknowledgment that we are lost by ourselves and cannot do it alone.

God often waits for us to seek His help before offering it.

- Write your own plea for mercy.

- How might you become less self-sufficient?

- How are you struggling for control instead of trusting God?

The Spiritual Journey

- Following the guidance of Matthew 7:7, what are some of your prayerful petitions?

"Ask and it will be given to you; seek and you will find; knock and the door will be opened to you." (Matthew 7:7)

Move deeper into friendship with God

As we move deeper on the spiritual journey, our friendship with God becomes increasingly intimate. We move in and out of five stages of friendship at different times in our lives: stranger, acquaintance, casual friend, close friend, and soul mate.

- Referring to the descriptions of the following categories in *Relationships of Grace,* which best describes your relationship with God?

_____ Stranger
_____ Acquaintance
_____ Casual friend
_____ Close friend
_____ Soul mate

"Don't bargain with God. Be direct. Ask for what you need. This isn't a cat-and-mouse, hide-and-seek game we're in. If your child asks for bread, do you trick him with sawdust? If he asks for fish, do you scare him with a live snake on his plate? As bad as you are, you wouldn't think of such a thing. You're at least decent to your own children. So don't you think the God who conceived you in love will be even better?" (Matthew 7:7-11 MSG)

- The key for moving deeper into friendship with God, and becoming a soul mate in union with God, is found in Jeremiah 29:13–14. Complete the passage to discover the key: "Yes, when you get serious about finding me and

_____,

I'll make sure you won't be disappointed." (Jeremiah 29:13–14 MSG)

- Is God your number one priority, before everyone and everything else?

" When you call on me, when you come and pray to me, I'll listen. When you come looking for me, you'll find me. Yes, when you get serious about finding me and want it more than anything else, I'll make sure you won't be disappointed." (Jeremiah 29:13–14 MSG)

- If not, who and what are you putting before God?

Relationships of Grace Workbook

Nurture your relationship

"Be joyful always."
(1 Thessalonians 5:16)

How can the promise of 1 Thessalonians 5:16 to "be joyful always" become a reality? Nurture your relationship with God. Move deeper into union with God, moment to moment, through choice.

Joy is a fruit.

- List a fear, a sorrow, and a recurring envy.

- Explain how putting God at the center of your life would ease your fear, sorry, and envy.

For any relationship to thrive, it must be nurtured. Neglect it, for any reason—including busyness, no matter how virtuous—and the relationship suffers.

Relationship with God is no different.

If you don't replenish the well, it will run dry. Pray. Serve. Read and listen to inspirational material. Practice solitude. Observe the hand of God in everyday life. Visit with God anywhere and everywhere. And move deeper into relationship with Him.

- Are you willing to commit and make God *the* priority in your life? Share your thoughts below.

The Spiritual Journey

Centering Prayer

The temptation for many of us is to spend our prayer time doing a lot of talking, but not much listening. It's tough to hear God when we are speaking.

During centering prayer, God talks. You sit in silence and listen. Centering prayer helps you empty yourself of the noise of an external world and be filled with the presence of God. When you are struggling with a problem, the deep inner-silence of centering prayer helps you hear the voice of God as He shines a lamp unto your feet and directs your path.

Hearing the Whisper

Centering prayer helps you hear the whispers of God. It brings you into a state of stillness and awakens you to God's presence, allowing you to hear the divine guidance reverberating within.

- When you pray, do you listen?

In the ongoing debate of quantity time versus quality time, quantity is key when it comes to prayer. What's important is not praying the perfect prayer, but that we pray. The real issue regarding prayer is not whether prayer should be taken out of public schools, but whether it has been taken out of our hearts.

Prayer is the primary means for establishing a relationship with God. Our connection moves past God of the foxhole to friend. We experience God through our hearts rather than relying solely on knowledge and doctrine.

- How often do you pray?

Relationships of Grace Workbook

- If you do not pray as often as you would like, how can you make more time for prayer?

Tranquil Waters

Centering prayer helps you journey inward, past the choppy waters of everyday life, to the tranquility within. You are freed to enjoy God's presence in calmer waters. It provides the opportunity for spiritual renewal and a peaceful time out from the noise of an external world. You move beyond thoughts, activity, and emotional turmoil into the presence of God.

As you enter into the fullness of the divine presence, you are emptied of some of the emotional baggage you may be carrying. Old wounds begin to heal. It is easier to keep problems in perspective. An emotional upset may seem less significant after twenty minutes in centering prayer.

- When you experience an emotional upset this week, take a time out for twenty minutes of centering prayer. Note your level of emotional turmoil before and after your centering prayer session.

Personal Experience

Centering prayer is not a relaxation technique, although relaxation is a benefit. While centered, as with all types of prayer, you enter into relationship with God.

The difference between secular meditation and centering prayer is one of resting versus resting *in God*.

Practice centering prayer

- Choose a sacred word or phrase: for example, *peace, Lord, love, God is love.* You do not need to write this down.

120

The Spiritual Journey

- Repeat your sacred phrase effortlessly. Do not concentrate or work at it, just gently repeat it. When you reach a state of stillness, sit in silence in the presence of God. This is a time for you to listen, not talk, to God. If you are struggling with a problem, gently ask for guidance. Then listen for the response. If your mind wanders, effortlessly return to your sacred phrase until you reach a state of stillness. Thoughts will come and go, especially during times of stress. Do not fight them or struggle to make your mind go blank. If a distracting thought is persistent, write it down on a piece of paper to release it, or think of a visual image such as a river to carry it away.

For some people, the effect of centering prayer is dramatic from the start. Others find sitting quietly difficult at first. A friend claimed it was the longest five minutes of her life when she tried it. You will become more comfortable sitting in stillness the more you practice. As you move deeper into the presence of God, you will find the deep silence is full and rich.

- Choose a regular time so it becomes part of your daily routine. Twenty minutes twice a day—once in the morning before you start your day and again in late afternoon to carry you through the rest of the evening—is the guidance I received. Experiment to see what works for you. Some people prefer a longer session in the morning. If you find these timelines to be impossible, do what works. Any amount of time is better than none. What works best for you?

- Choose a regular place for prayer: among the pillows on your bed, in the corner of an unused room, on a chair in the family room. The time and place should be quiet and free of interruptions. Some get up early before others awaken. Some wait until after the children go to school. A friend places a sign on the door to let her husband know it is her quiet time and she does not want to be disturbed. Where can you sit quietly, comfortably, and without interruptions?

Relationships of Grace Workbook

Experience God's presence throughout the day

"Pray continually."
(1 Thessalonians 5:17)

- How often does 1 Thessalonians 5:17 instruct us to pray?

Centering prayers said during your regular prayer time are maintenance prayers.

For a deeper relationship with God, centering prayers can also be said throughout the day, not just during a regular quiet time.

- Throughout the week, try to experience God's presence by silently repeating a sacred phrase as you go about your daily routine. Compare the days when you experience God's presence throughout the day with those when you do not.

- Try and practice another form of centering prayer this week: the emergency fix. The emergency fix is a quick form of centering prayer said during times of crises and emotional upsets to calm you down and bring you back into God's presence. Silently repeat a short, sacred phrase or passage of Scripture anytime you are emotionally upset. Emergency fixes can be said throughout the day to bring you back to center. Note your experiences below.

The Spiritual Journey

Gratitude and Grace

Writing down the things you are grateful for takes the focus off what you don't have and helps you appreciate the things you do have. Journaling your gratitude on a regular basis and whenever you are struggling with self-pity is transforming.

– Journal your gratitude by completing the following sentences.

- I am grateful for . . .

- I am grateful for . . .

- I am grateful for . . .

- I am grateful for . . .

- I am grateful for . . .

- I am grateful for . . .

- I am grateful for . . .

Relationships of Grace Workbook

- I am grateful for . . .

- I am grateful for . . .

- Notice how you feel after you have written down the things for which you are grateful. Do you feel . . . grateful?

As the Wall Fell

A group of people who won the lottery participated in a study of the effects of winning on happiness five years later. The results indicated the lottery had no effect on happiness. People who were happy before winning were happy after. Unhappy people were still unhappy.

In a Nazi concentration camp, one man asked another how he could kneel and give thanks to God. The man replied, "I told God I am thankful I am not like them."

Gratitude is the result of internal condition, not external circumstance. It is accepting what is instead of dwelling on what is not.

Two things keep us from being grateful: insisting things happen our way instead of trusting God's plan, and disconnecting the gift from the Giver.

Bask in graceful surroundings

- Do you find yourself coveting the things you do not have and taking for granted what you do have? Explain.

"He tends his flock like a shepherd: He gathers the lambs in his arms and carries them close to his heart." (Isaiah 40:11)

- What is the hope of Isaiah 40:11?

The Spiritual Journey

- Why don't you need to be afraid according to Isaiah 43:5?

"Do not be afraid, for I am with you." (Isaiah 43:5)

- According to Acts 17:25 NLT, God gives you everything you _____.

God "satisfies every need there is." (Acts 17:25 NLT)

To be drawn into the graceful life, it is important to understand two things: God gives you everything you *need*, and *everything* comes from God. Discontent is the result of chasing after what you want instead of resting in what you need—which has been given to you.

Trust God's plan

- Do you struggle with ingratitude? Explain.

- Who or what do you take for granted?

- What are you struggling to control that keeps you from being grateful?

- What did fleas teach Corrie ten Boom about gratitude according to the story in the "Trust God's Plan section of *Relationships of Grace*?

- What are the fleas in your life?

Relationships of Grace Workbook

- How might the fleas in your life be part of God's plan?

"Give thanks in all circumstances."
(1 Thessalonians 5:18)

- Complete this sentence from 1 Thessalonians 5:18: "Give thanks in _____ circumstances."

How do you "give thanks in all circumstances"? By trusting in God's plan.

Observe the hand of God

God "gives all men life and breath and everything else."
(Acts 17:25)

- What comes from God according to Acts 17:25?

- Personalize the teaching of Acts 17:25 by writing down specific things in your life that are gifts from God.

Gratitude is the fruit of becoming aware of the blessings of grace that surround you and acknowledging the source of all gifts. To be ungrateful is to disregard the Giver.

Notice the graceful beauty of a rose, trees in autumn, and a newborn baby.

Watch as your table is filled with daily bread.

Trust your future to the Planner of it.

Observe the parting of the clouds.

If you have ever flown on a stormy day, you have likely noticed the sun shining above the clouds.

The rays of grace always shine. God is always at work and always with you, even during storms.

Notice. Watch. Trust. Observe. And bear the fruit: gratitude.

126

Solitude

It's tough to take time out from the busyness of everyday life to just *be*.

Aching to Seek

Loving family and friends surround me. And yet, sometimes, the dull ache of loneliness sets in. Sometimes it comes when I've been writing for a while and need to get out. But I've experienced the feelings in the middle of a crowd.

The ache, I've learned, only masquerades as pain. It is really a seeking. The urging is not for activity and crowds, but for solitude. The emptiness is a yearning for fullness that can only be experienced deep in the presence of God.

I have felt alone in a crowd, but I have never felt lonely in the solitude of One.

Eugene Peterson, author of *The Message,* wrote, "Busyness is the enemy of spirituality."

- We are created to seek. When we neglect our inborn hunger for God, we try and fill the void in other ways. How do you attempt to fill the emptiness?

- What substitutes and addictions keep you from experiencing the fullness of God?

- How does busyness keep you from the fullness of solitude with God?

Relationships of Grace Workbook

- How does fear keep you busy with activity, leaving little time for solitude?

Solitary Delight

Solitude is a state of profound stillness—a thundering, inner silence. It helps you shut out the noise of an external world. This frees you to commune with God and hear His voice. You move from *doing* to *being*. It is a wonderful way to practice spiritual renewal and open your heart to the blessings of grace.

Solitude provides refuge from the madness. It helps you experience peace in the midst of chaos. Inner turmoil fades into a rich, inner fullness. It gives you a chance to take a vacation from your problems for a while. The serenity of going inward to reach your inner sanctuary is not boring or lonesome.

Experience solitude anywhere, anytime

"Be cheerful no matter what; pray all the time; thank God no matter what happens."
(1 Thessalonians 5:16-17 MSG)

- What does 1 Thessalonians 5:16-17 ask of us?

Our only hope for constant joy, prayer, and gratitude is to experience God's presence—continually.

Practicing solitude anywhere, anytime will help you bring more joy, prayer, and gratitude into your life.

Solitude is an internal condition, not an external circumstance. You can experience it in the middle of a crowd and not experience it alone in the wilderness. Solitude is not synonymous with being alone, although seclusion is a wonderful way to experience solitude.

- List times throughout the day when you can experience solitude. For example, laying in bed at night, before getting up in the morning, doing the dishes, driving to work, etc.

The Spiritual Journey

Schedule time in your day for solitude. Several times a year, devote a larger block of time for spiritual renewal—a morning, an afternoon, a day.

Practice solitude anywhere: an empty bedroom, by a mountain stream, at the beach, on a park bench near a favorite tree in the middle of the city, in the car waiting to pick your child up from school.

Be

Solitude is a state of being; describing how to practice it is an incongruity. Nonetheless, a brief depiction is in order.

Simply, be in the presence of God. Listen and see much. Talk little. Pray. Read Scripture. Listen to inspirational music. Walk in nature. Stand in awe at the wonder of God's masterpiece. Allow yourself to be immersed in peace and grace.

- List some specific ways in which you can practice solitude.

- Practice solitude this week and describe your experience.

CHAPTER SIX

Growing Like a Child

"Who gets the highest rank in God's kingdom?" the disciples asked Jesus. (Matthew 18:1) In our material world, this would likely be the privileged, the accomplished, winners of awards, and those in positions of power and control.

- What was Jesus' response according to Matthew 18:2-4?

- The Amplified Bible parenthetically describes a child as trusting, lowly, loving, and forgiving. How would you describe a child?

"The disciples came to Jesus asking, 'Who gets the highest rank in God's kingdom?'" (Matthew 18:1 MSG)

"He called a little child and had him stand among them. And he said: 'I tell you the truth, unless you change and become like little children, you will never enter the kingdom of heaven. Therefore, whoever humbles himself like this child is the greatest in the kingdom of heaven.'" (Matthew 18:2-4)

As we have journeyed through the pages of this book, I am learning how to become more childlike. And since you are still with me, I suspect the same is true for you.

For as you grow in grace, you become more childlike. I hope we are growing together—humble, like a child.

- Let's spend some time celebrating how you have grown throughout the pages of this study. Share your thoughts as you contemplate the following questions.

- How has your relationship with God grown?

Relationships of Grace Workbook

- Do you know God better than when you began this study?

- Do you know how incredible you are? Do you understand— really know in your heart—you are of value because God created you?

- What are some of the blessings of grace given to you?

- Do you understand that your value as a human being is a gift of grace?

- How do you allow God's power—the power of grace—to work through you?

- How has opening your heart to grace helped you become more receptive to God's will?

Growing Like a Child

- Are you leaning on God more and asking Him for help?

- Are you relinquishing self-sufficiency and recognizing your dependence on God?

- What are some examples of when you entrusted the outcome to God?

- How have you been transformed?

- How is the masterpiece being unveiled as you let go of the mask?

- Are you fearing less and loving more by trusting God?

Relationships of Grace Workbook

- Are you experiencing less frustration by moving away from "I want what I want" and trusting God to provide what you need?

- What problems have turned into opportunities as you sought grace in the darkness?

- What are some examples of how you have become a moonbeam of grace by administering grace to others?

- How are you relying on the power and wisdom of the Holy Spirit?

- How are you accepting other people and circumstances more, and trying to control them less?

- Are you experiencing passion, purpose, and meaning by living God's plan for you?

Growing Like a Child

- How are you using your talents to serve others?

May many graceful moments satisfy the longings of your heart.

Always remember this: You create loving relationships, love yourself, and live with meaning by choosing to open your heart to grace.

Grace is God's part.

Choice is yours.

Choose to open your heart to grace, moment by moment. Develop an awareness of the blessings of grace given to you. Receive the gift that is always present and always free. Everything good in life flows from God's grace.

Enter into a relationship with God. Allow God's power to work through you. Let God work His will in you. Ask Him for help. Relinquish self-sufficiency. Recognize your dependence on, surrender to, and trust in God. And leave the outcome to Him.

Instead of knowing about God, know God. (Hosea 6:6) And experience a transformation.

As you put down the mask and trudge through the mud, watch as the masterpiece is unveiled. I hope a renewed understanding of your worth helps you fear less and love more. Your value is a gift of grace; you are valuable because God created you. If you find yourself weary, remember to move away from "I want what I want" and trust in God to provide what you need. Turn problems into opportunities by seeking grace in the darkness.

I am confident you are becoming a moonbeam of grace and administering grace to others. I trust you are learning to rely on the power and wisdom of the Holy Spirit. I presume you are accepting other people and circumstances more, and trying to control them less.

May you live a life full of passion, purpose, and meaning by living God's plan for you. Draw on the unique talents given to you. Treasure the journey without being too anxious about the outcome.

My hope is you continue to grow—humble, like a child.

My prayer is that your life is full of meaning and that you experience relationships of grace.

"I want you to be merciful; I don't want your sacrifices. I want you to know God; that's more important than burnt offerings." (Hosea 6:6 NLT)

On the Wings of Grace*

Behind my mask and mortal schemes,
Are tears and fears and broken dreams.

If I seek, will You take my hand,
And dance with me across the land?

Today I come on bended knee,
Surrender and trust in You for me.

Come rest upon my broken heart,
Transform me into Your work of art.

World of wonder, from earth to sky,
On the wings of grace, we fly.

Chris Karcher
Relationships of Grace

---

* A free print that contains this poem and accompanying artwork is available for a limited time at
www.RelationshipsOfGrace.com

About the Author

Chris Karcher has enjoyed a distinguished career as author, professional speaker, and manager of multimillion-dollar programs while working in industry.

Chris is the author of three books, ten technical documents, and two adult Sunday school curriculums. Her books include *Amazing Things I Know About You, Relationships of Grace,* and *Relationships of Grace Workbook*. She is currently writing her next book *Relationships of Grace Miracles*. Chris teaches adult Sunday school. She is the author of class curriculums *Creating Loving Relationships: Loving God, Others, and Self* and *Majestic Grace* and coauthor of *Christianity 101*. Chris served on the Board of Directors for the National Speakers Association Utah chapter.

Chris has been married to her husband, Dave, for twenty-five years. They have a wonderful daughter, Erin.

Free Offers*

Visit www.RelationshipsOfGrace.com for the following free resources:

- A set of worksheets in journal format containing selected self-reflective questions from *Relationships of Grace* and *Relationships of Grace Workbook*

- A print and accompanying artwork of the poem *On the Wings of Grace*

- The *Relationships of Grace* newsletter

*Please note offers subject to change

Share Your Story in Our Next Book

You are invited to submit a story, anecdote, or quotation for possible inclusion in our next book. This may be your own original material or something you have read that was written by someone else. Both the author and contributor will be acknowledged. A seventy-five-word biography of the author will be included. Multiple submissions are welcome.

For *Relationships of Grace Miracles*, two types of stories are needed. First, stories about gifts of grace—miracles, twists of fate, everyday blessings, and divine incidents disguised as ordinary events and coincidences. Second, stories for each section in the table of contents at the front of this book (e.g., The Naked Choice, Loving Yourself, From Fear to Love, etc.). Please indicate the applicable section with your submission. If your story fits into more than one section, write the story once with a brief explanation of how the story could be adapted to multiple sections.

Stories should encourage and inspire readers through emotion or humor. Suggested length is 350 to 1500 words. Please use stories, illustrations, and metaphors to teach. Avoid preaching and religious jargon. Stories should reach across denominational boundaries.

For complete guidelines and the submission deadline, please visit our website, send a fax or email, or mail your request with a stamped, self-addressed envelope to:

Relationships of Grace
P.O. Box 1043
Layton, Utah 84041-1043
Fax: 801-547-0928
www.RelationshipsOfGrace.com
guidelines@relationshipsofgrace.com

You will only hear from us if your story is selected. Due to time constraints, submissions will not be returned.

The preferred method to submit a story is a Word or Word Perfect file sent as an attachment via email to:
miracles@RelationshipsOfGrace.com
Or, you may fax or mail a hardcopy as indicated above.

Amazing Things I Know About You by Chris Karcher

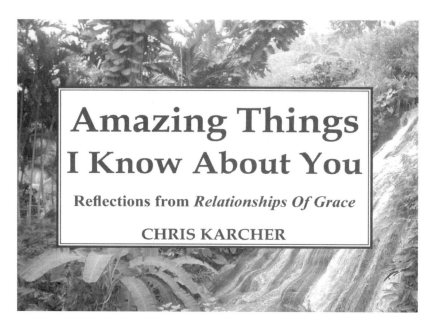

ISBN 1-932356-51-7

You are amazing. Discover the real reason you are of value; learn how to unveil the masterpiece within through these reflections from *Relationships of Grace*. Whether for your own personal enrichment or as a gift for a friend, *Amazing Things I Know About You* shares inspirational messages of encouragement and hope.

**Available from selected bookstores, or
Call 1-877-GET-GRACE (1-877-438-4722), or
Visit www.RelationshipsOfGrace.com**

Relationships of Grace by Chris Karcher

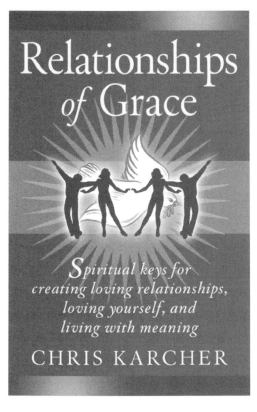

"Delightful stories . . . powerful lessons."
—**Jack Canfield**, co-creator of *Chicken Soup for the Soul*®

"A **Max Lucado** writing style . . ."
—**Lea Ann Lobb, KUTV, Salt Lake City, Television News Anchor**

"Grace-full."
—**John Ortberg**, author of
Everybody's Normal Till You Get To Know Them

"Universal spiritual truths . . ."
—**Foster Cline**, co-author of *Parenting with Love and Logic*

"A warm, wonderful, inspiring book . . ."
—**Brian Tracy**, author of *Create Your Own Future*

"Incredible . . . a gripping intensity . . ."
—**Glenna Salsbury, CSP, CPAE Speaker Hall of Fame
Past President National Speakers Association
Author of** *The Art of the Fresh Start*

"Inspires us . . ."
—**LeAnn Thieman**, coauthor of
**Chicken Soup for the Christian Woman's Soul
and Chicken Soup for the Nurse's Soul**

"A magnificent job . . ."
—**Naomi Rhode, CSP, CPAE Speaker Hall of Fame
Past President National Speakers Association**

Trade paperback	ISBN 1-932356-51-7
Workbook	ISBN 1-932356-53-3
CD, abridged	ISBN 1-932356-20-7
Audiocassette, abridged	ISBN 1-932356-21-5

Change From the Inside Out

With the wisdom of Scott Peck's *The Road Less Traveled* and the masterful storytelling and insight of Max Lucado's *In the Grip of Grace, Relationships of Grace* reveals how you can create loving relationships, love yourself, and live with meaning through the transforming power of grace. Discover the exciting truth in this riveting book as you explore the essential element of intimacy and learn the secret for dealing with difficult people. Explore the miracle and mystery of the timeless spiritual teaching of grace applied to everyday life. Anyone who feels spiritually disconnected and wants to improve his or her relationships will benefit from this enlightening book. You will discover how to:

- Know God
- Love yourself
- Create loving relationships with family, friends, and colleagues
- Overcome fear, worry, stress, addiction, or a bad habit
- Live with meaning
- Open your heart to grace

**Available from selected bookstores, or
Call 1-877-GET-GRACE (1-877-438-4722), or
Visit www.RelationshipsOfGrace.com**

For information about *Relationships of Grace*
speeches, retreats, and products,
or to join our mailing list,
please contact:

Relationships of Grace
P.O. Box 1043
Layton, Utah 84041-1043

www.RelationshipsOfGrace.com
news@RelationshipsOfGrace.com
Fax: 801-547-0928